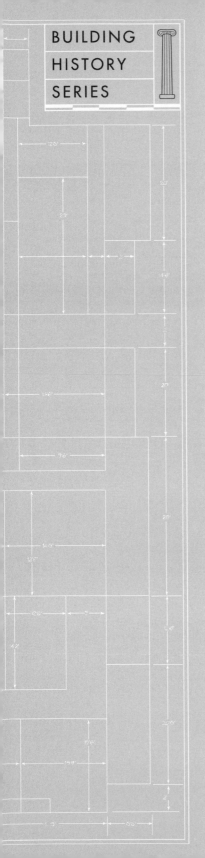

ROMAN
ROADS AND
AQUEDUCTS

BUILDING
HISTORY
SERIES

ROMAN
ROADS AND
AQUEDUCTS

by Don Nardo

Lucent Books, Inc., San Diego, California

Library of Congress Cataloging-in-Publication Data

Nardo, Don, 1947–
  Roman roads and aqueducts / by Don Nardo
    p. cm. — (Building history series)
Includes bibliographical references and index.
Summary: Describes the construction of roads and aqueducts in
ancient Rome, life and customs along the roads, water distribution
and aqueduct maintenance, and the building of bridges.
  ISBN 1-56006-721-7 (alk. paper)
  1. Roads, Roman—Juvenile literature. 2. Bridges—Rome—Juvenile
literature. 3. Aqueducts—Rome—Juvenile literature. [1. Roads, Roman.
2. Bridges—Rome. 3. Aqueducts—Rome. 4. Rome—Civilization.] I. Title.
II. Series.
  DG28 .N37 2001
  388. 1'0937—dc21

                                                              00-009155

Printed in the U.S.A.

Contents

Foreword

Throughout history, as civilizations have evolved and prospered, each has produced unique buildings and architectural styles. Combining the need for both utility and artistic expression, a society's buildings, particularly its large-scale public structures, often reflect the individual character traits that distinguish it from other societies. In a very real sense, then, buildings express a society's values and unique characteristics in tangible form. As scholar Anita Abramovitz comments in her book *People and Spaces*, "Our ways of living and thinking—our habits, needs, fear of enemies, aspirations, materialistic concerns, and religious beliefs—have influenced the kinds of spaces that we build and that later surround and include us."

That specific types and styles of structures constitute an outward expression of the spirit of an individual people or era can be seen in the diverse ways that various societies have built palaces, fortresses, tombs, churches, government buildings, sports arenas, public works, and other such monuments. The ancient Greeks, for instance, were a supremely rational people who originated Western philosophy and science, including the atomic theory and the realization that the earth is a sphere. Their public buildings, epitomized by Athens's magnificent Parthenon temple, were equally rational, emphasizing order, harmony, reason, and above all, restraint.

By contrast, the Romans, who conquered and absorbed the Greek lands, were a highly practical people preoccupied with acquiring and wielding power over others. The Romans greatly admired and readily copied elements of Greek architecture, but modified and adapted them to their own needs. "Roman genius was called into action by the enormous practical needs of a world empire," wrote historian Edith Hamilton. "Rome met them magnificently. Buildings tremendous, indomitable, amphitheaters where eighty thousand could watch a spectacle, baths where three thousand could bathe at the same time."

In medieval Europe, God heavily influenced and motivated the people, and religion permeated all aspects of society, molding people's worldviews and guiding their everyday actions. That spiritual mindset is reflected in the most important medieval structure—the Gothic cathedral—which, in a sense, was a model of heavenly cities. As scholar Anne Fremantle so elegantly phrases it, the cathedrals were "harmonious elevations of stone and glass reaching up to heaven to seek and receive the light [of God]."

Our more secular modern age, in contrast, is driven by the realities of a global economy, advanced technology, and mass communications. Responding to the needs of international trade and the growth of cities housing millions of people, today's builders construct engineering marvels, among them towering skyscrapers of steel and glass, mammoth marine canals, and huge and elaborate rapid transit systems, all of which would have left their ancestors, even the Romans, awestruck.

In examining some of humanity's greatest edifices, Lucent Books' Building History series recognizes this close relationship between a society's historical character and its buildings. Each volume in the series begins with a historical sketch of the people who erected the edifice, exploring their major achievements as well as the beliefs, customs, and societal needs that dictated the variety, functions, and styles of their buildings. A detailed explanation of how the selected structure was conceived, designed, and built, to the extent that this information is known, makes up the majority of the volume.

Each volume in the Lucent Building History series also includes several special features that are useful tools for additional research. A chronology of important dates gives students an overview, at a glance, of the evolution and use of the structure described. Sidebars create a broader context by adding further details on some of the architects, engineers, and construction tools, materials, and methods that made each structure a reality, as well as the social, political, and/or religious leaders and movements that inspired its creation. Useful maps help the reader locate the nations, cities, streets, and individual structures mentioned in the text; and numerous diagrams and pictures illustrate tools and devices that bring to life various stages of construction. Finally, each volume contains two bibliographies, one for student research, the other listing works the author consulted in compiling the book.

Taken as a whole, these volumes, covering diverse ancient and modern structures, constitute not only a valuable research tool, but also a tribute to the human spirit, a fascinating exploration of the dreams, skills, ingenuity, and dogged determination of the great peoples who shaped history.

INTRODUCTION

When ancient Roman civilization declined and fell in the fifth and sixth centuries A.D., it left behind numerous pieces of itself. Some of these survivals of a vanished empire and way of life take the form of cultural ideas and institutions; others are of a more physical nature. Both made an indelible impression on the later culture of Europe and those lands and peoples who sprang from European stock. In the realm of ideas, for example, the contribution of Roman law to European law courts and justice systems, including such concepts as trial by jury, impartial justice, and unwritten "laws of nature," is enormous to say the least.

Europe is also the proud custodian of Rome's physical remains, a profusion of ruins that continue to draw millions of tourists from around the globe annually. These magnificent remnants of ancient Rome's infrastructure (basic communal facilities) attest in no uncertain terms that the Romans were great builders, overall the most prolific, efficient, and practical in the ancient world. Indeed, the word *practical* perhaps best sums up the driving force behind much of Roman achievement, for the true Roman artist was not the painter, sculptor, or poet, but rather the engineer. "Roman genius was called into action by the enormous practical needs of a world empire," writes noted scholar Edith Hamilton.[1] Rome met these needs appropriately and impressively by producing a vast network of roads for the swift transport of armies and trade goods; miles of aqueducts, channels that supplied life-sustaining water to hundreds of cities; as well as giant racetracks, arenas (like the Colosseum), and public baths, each of which accommodated thousands of people at a time.

It is important to emphasize that the Romans did not invent roads, aqueducts, and racetracks. More often than not, in fact, they borrowed their architectural ideas from the Greeks and other ancient peoples. Yet far from being mere copiers, the Romans possessed an amazing talent for combining foreign ideas with their own native concepts and skills to produce structures suited to their own practical needs. And even those structures that the Romans adopted with little or no change reached grand heights of achievement in size, efficiency, durability, and sheer numbers that far surpassed any known before. The results, Hamilton movingly puts it, were

8

bridges and aqueducts that spanned wide rivers and traversed great spaces with a beautiful, sure precision of soaring arches and massive piers [vertical supports]. And always along with them the mighty Roman road, a monument of dogged, unconquerable human effort, huge stone jointed to huge stone, marching on and on irresistibly, through unknown hostile forests, over ramparts of mountains, across sun-baked deserts, to the very edges of the habitable world. That is the true art of Rome.[2]

These two great vestiges and symbols of ancient Rome—roads and aqueducts—had a number of points in common. Both were large-scale and important public works supplying the Roman people with essential services, for example. And both stimulated the

The remains of the vast Colosseum, the most famous of all Roman structures, stand as mute testimony to the talents and accomplishments of the ancient Romans as builders.

Across this impressive double arcade of arches in Spain once flowed the life-giving water for the inhabitants of a large town.

growth of population in a given area by making the transport of large quantities of life-giving food and water into that area cheap and practical. In this way, says historian Lionel Casson, these works "determined where many of the great urban centers of Europe would be."[3] Roman roads and aqueducts also had in common that, because of their tremendous importance to society, their construction was supervised by high public officials. Sometimes the same men built both kinds of structures; for instance, Rome's first major paved road and its first aqueduct were both initiated by the noted public works commissioner Appius Claudius Caecus, and in the same year (312 B.C.). Moreover, both roads and aqueducts often followed the same routes through the countryside, sometimes running side by side for miles.

Finally, and significantly from a structural standpoint, both roads and aqueducts utilized bridges in short but crucial segments of their total lengths. Indeed, writes noted civil engineer and historian Colin O'Connor, "Bridges and roads go together, for it is the roads which require the bridges, and the bridges make possible the roads."[4] Similarly, says O'Connor, "It is impossible to speak of bridges without referring . . . to aqueducts also. The most famous of all 'bridges' is, in fact, an aqueduct—the Pont du Gard [in what is now southern France]."[5] From a visual as well as an engineering standpoint, Roman bridges remain the most impressive and memorable parts of the roads and aqueducts. As French architectural historian Jean-Pierre Adam puts it:

> Bridges, for roads as much as for aqueducts, represent the most spectacular construction works. They are

also the most significant because of the place they occupy in a landscape or an urban environment and because many of those that have survived are still in use today.[6]

This astonishing fact—that some of the bridges and roads the Romans built so long ago are still in use—is in itself sufficient reason to examine these imposing relics of a truly remarkable people.

How the Romans Constructed Their Roads

The Romans were not the first people in the ancient world to build large-scale roads. A powerful Near Eastern empire, that of the Assyrians, constructed an impressive network of roads in the late second millennium B.C., well before the city-state called Rome was established. The well-maintained Assyrian roads were mostly made of dirt. But the short sections that approached temples and other important buildings were paved, consisting of a layer of bricks topped by large slabs of polished limestone. Later, in the sixth and fifth centuries B.C., another Near Eastern people, the Persians, inherited the Assyrian road system. The Persians greatly expanded and improved the old roads, and the Persian "Royal Road" stretched some sixteen hundred miles eastward from the Mediterranean coast to Persia's capital, Susa. About this highway, then a marvel of the world, the fifth-century B.C. Greek historian Herodotus wrote:

> At intervals all along the road are recognized stations, with excellent inns, and the road itself is safe to travel by, as it never leaves inhabited country. . . . Traveling at the rate of 150 furlongs [about 18 miles] a day, a man will take just ninety days to make the journey [from one end of the road to the other].[7]

The Greeks and Etruscans (an early Italian people who lived just north of Rome) also built many roads, and the techniques they used directly influenced Roman road builders.

As impressive as these early road systems were for their time, however, they paled in comparison to those built by the Romans. First, although a large number of Roman roads were made of dirt, a good many were expertly paved and graded for great distances. Most of these proved far more durable than the roads of earlier peoples, so much so that some of the Roman versions are still in use today. Moreover, the sheer size of the Roman road system dwarfed all others constructed in the world until the twentieth century. By about A.D. 300, the Roman Empire had over 370 at least partially paved major highways, totaling some 53,000 miles in all; thousands of smaller roads branched outward from these main roads, creating a total mileage, in all likelihood, in the hundreds of thousands. An engineering achievement of the first order, the Roman road system was also "one of profound significance," says Lionel Casson:

> It enabled her rulers to establish and maintain the most durable empire in European history; it set the lines along which traders, priests, and soldiers would carry the seeds of change in Western civilization. . . . Only a rich and powerful state whose authority stretched unchallenged far and wide could have carried out the task.[8]

THE VARIOUS KINDS OF ROMAN ROADS

Roman roads were not all of one type. Like people do today, the Romans built various kinds of roads, with numerous names and

Major Roman roads were often lined with tombs and other grave markers, as depicted in this nineteenth-century illustration of the famous Appian Way.

classifications. One the more familiar road names, *via*, meant a road (or sometimes a city street) large enough for two vehicles to pass each other; this is the term most commonly applied to major highways, such as the Via Appia (or Appian Way), the road begun by Appius Claudius. The general term for a city street was *vicus*, while a very narrow street or alleyway was an *angiportus* and a street with an unusually steep slope was a *clivus*. The term *agger*, which meant an embankment or mound, was often applied to a road built atop a raised mound or causeway. And a single-lane country road, usually originating as a trackway for cattle and other animals, and almost always of dirt rather than paved, was called an *actus*. Still another term, *limes*, was used to describe a small road, usually of dirt, that marked a boundary line between two pieces of property or two territorial regions.

In addition to these and other individual names for roads, the Romans had general road classifications. A first-century A.D. Roman surveyor named Siculus Flaccus wrote a treatise that lists the four official classes of road recognized in his day. In this breakdown, based on which party or parties bore the financial responsibility for the road, the first class consisted of public highways (*viae publicae*). "Public highways," says Flaccus,

> [are] constructed at state [i.e., government] expense, [and] bear the names of their builders, and they are under the charge of administrators, who have the work done by contractors; for some of these [major] roads, the landowners in the area are required, too, from time to time, to pay a fixed sum.[9]

Note that Flaccus uses the general term "administrator" to describe those who built and maintained the major public roads. Actually, the type of administrator varied from one era to another and also according to the task performed. For example, during the Roman Republic, the era (and government) lasting from about 509 to 30 B.C., high government officials called censors (*censores*) were charged with initiating road-building projects. (Among a censor's tasks were taking a census of citizens and property, keeping an eye on public morals, leasing public land, deciding on new construction projects, and awarding the contracts for these projects; so a censor like the famous Appius Claudius can be thought of as the Roman equivalent of a com-

GRACCHUS THE ROAD BUILDER

In his biography of the Roman statesman Gaius Gracchus (ca. 153–121 B.C.), the first-century A.D. Greek writer Plutarch included a brief description of Gracchus's noteworthy achievements in road building (quoted here from John Dryden's translation).

His most special exertions were given to constructing the roads, which he was careful to make beautiful and pleasant, as well as convenient. They were drawn by his directions through the fields, exactly in a straight line, partly paved with hewn stone, and partly laid with solid masses of gravel. When he met with any deep valleys or watercourses crossing the line, he either caused them to be filled up with rubbish, or bridges to be built over them, so well leveled that . . . the work presented one uniform and beautiful prospect. Besides this, he caused the roads to be all divided into miles . . . and erected pillars of stone [*miliaria*] to signify the distance from one place to another. He likewise placed other stones at small distances from one another, on both sides of the way, by the help of which travelers might get easily on horseback without wanting a groom.

Gaius Gracchus, a social reformer who also built roads.

missioner of public works.) The tasks of resurfacing, cleaning, and otherwise maintaining public roads during the Republic were the job of magistrates called *aediles*. The *aediles* had charge of maintaining all public works and also oversaw marketplaces and public games.

In 20 B.C., at the start of the Roman Empire, the era (and government) lasting from 30 B.C. to A.D. 476, Augustus, the first Roman emperor, set up a special board of curators—the *curatores viarum*—to manage public highways in Italy, the Roman heartland. Thereafter, as a rule, one curator was responsible

A statue of the first emperor, Augustus, who set up a board of curators to manage the road system.

for the upkeep and policing of one major road. In Rome's outlying provinces, which multiplied in number during the Empire, the governors of those provinces had overall charge of roads; customarily, a governor contacted a local community and ordered its magistrates either to repair an existing road or to construct a new one in the vicinity of that community.

The second official class of roads, according to Flaccus, consisted of the strategic or military roads (*viae militares*). As indicated by their name, these roads were built by Roman soldiers and at the army's expense. The first major roads the Romans built, the military roads were initially used almost exclusively by troops making their way to distant battlefields, but in time these highways came into general public use.

The other two general classes of road Flaccus lists are local roads (*actus*) and private roads (*privatae*):

There are in addition local roads which, after branching off from the main highway, go off across the country and, often, lead to other public ways. They are built and maintained by the *pagi* [rural districts, each with a village as its administrative center], that is to say by the magistrates of the *pagi*, who usually see that landowners provide the work force, or rather hand to each landowner the job of looking after the stretch of road going over his land. . . . There is free movement along all these public ways. Finally, there are [road]ways leading across private estates that do not afford passage to everyone, but only to those who need to reach their fields. These ways lead off local roads. Sometimes too they fork off from roads belonging jointly to two landowners, who have come to an agreement to take charge of them at the edges of their estates and to share their upkeep.[10]

The Initial Steps in Building a Road

Another way the Romans classified their roads was by the ways these routes were surfaced. The term *via terrena*, for example, referred to a simple dirt road. A *via glarea strata*, on the other hand, had a more durable surface of gravel. More durable still was the surface of a *via silice strata*, a road or stretch of road paved with blocks of stone. By the first century B.C., most of the streets in the larger Roman cities were paved, as were large sections of the Via Appia and other major highways leading to and from the capital city, Rome.

Building a major paved road like the Via Appia was an expensive and time-consuming process that involved a number of systematic steps. The first of these was to lay out the proposed route,

work done by surveyors (*agrimensores* or *librators*). To lay out a roughly straight route from one point to another was easy if the two points were both in the line of sight, of course. But it was much more difficult when the two points were separated by tens or hundreds of miles of hilly, wooded countryside. The method Roman surveyors used to accomplish this feat is still not known for certain, but modern scholars have made some educated guesses. One popular scenario involves the use of fire beacons. "Although we have no reliable evidence," write scholars L. A. and J. A. Hamey,

Workers construct a street in this carving on the great column erected by the emperor Trajan.

it is very likely that a line of beacons was used, perhaps by night, but more probably at dawn or dusk. From any beacon it would be possible to see the next in each direction and by some process of laborious adjustment they would be moved into a straight line to form a primary alignment [straight line for the proposed road].[11]

Once they had established such a primary alignment, the surveyors laid out the route on the ground by driving wooden stakes at intervals. Of course, it was still not possible to lay out a perfectly straight route all the way because rivers, ravines, cliffs, and other natural obstacles sometimes got in the way. The problem of carrying the road across rivers and ravines could be solved by erecting bridges. But the best place to put a bridge (the shortest and therefore easiest and least expensive way across) did not always happen to lie within the road's primary, ideal alignment. In such cases, the surveyors took slight detours, so it was common for a road to jog east or west of the primary alignment for a few hundred feet or even for several miles; eventually, it would rejoin that alignment and reach its destination in what was overall the straightest and shortest possible route.

PREPARING THE ROADBED

After the surveyors had finished laying out the route, the actual construction of the road could begin. The tasks of clearing the route of boulders, trees, and other obstacles, as well as digging or otherwise preparing the roadbed itself, were done almost entirely by

ORDEAL IN A ROMAN TUNNEL

Although Roman roads most often skirted the bases and slopes of mountains, on occasion the builders excavated tunnels right through these obstacles. Of particular note was the spectacular 2,312-foot-long, 16-foot-high *crypta Neopolitana*, built near Naples in the late first century B.C. by one of the emperor Augustus's architects. In a letter to a friend (quoted here from C. D. N. Costa's translation) the first-century A.D. philosopher and playwright Seneca recalls his discomfort in passing through this engineering marvel.

[After enduring a mud-soaked overland walk] we then faced a sand-dusting in the Naples tunnel. Nothing is longer than that prison, nothing more gloomy than the torches [sold to travelers at the entrance] there, which intensify the darkness rather than enabling us to see through it. In any case, even if the place had any light, the dust would conceal it. Dust is a serious nuisance even in the open. You can imagine what it's like in that place, where it just eddies around, and since there's no ventilation, it settles on those who have stirred it up.

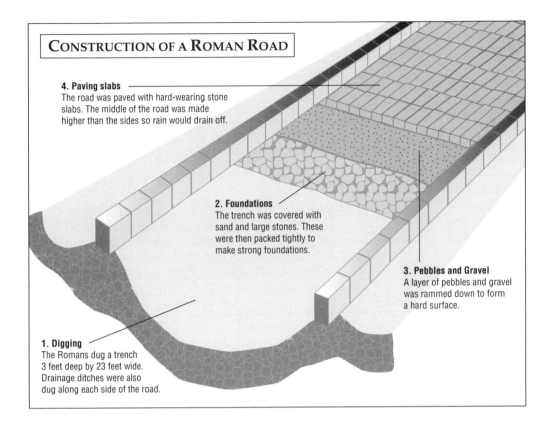

Construction of a Roman Road

4. Paving slabs
The road was paved with hard-wearing stone slabs. The middle of the road was made higher than the sides so rain would drain off.

2. Foundations
The trench was covered with sand and large stones. These were then packed tightly to make strong foundations.

3. Pebbles and Gravel
A layer of pebbles and gravel was rammed down to form a hard surface.

1. Digging
The Romans dug a trench 3 feet deep by 23 feet wide. Drainage ditches were also dug along each side of the road.

hand; not surprisingly, therefore, the construction stage was arduous and required the labor of hundreds of workers over the course of months and often years. In the earliest days of Roman road building, when the chief use of large roads was military, these workers were mostly soldiers. But over time, as the Roman road system expanded across the countryside, the soldiers were aided and sometimes replaced by civilians. Most of the latter were evidently free persons who lived in the various areas through which the new road passed; they either received wages or did the work as a way of satisfying part or all of their tax bills. Sometimes, slaves were also used. (Slaves were not necessarily markedly cheaper to use than freemen because the labor of Roman slaves was not free, as is often mistakenly assumed. Slaves not only had to be fed and housed, but most of them also received small wages for their efforts.)

The principal aim of these workers in preparing the roadbed was to ensure that the surface of the road would rest on material

A ROMAN DESCRIBES THE CONSTRUCTION OF A ROADBED

A rare eyewitness account of workers preparing the bed of a Roman road appears in the *Silvae*, by the first-century A.D. Roman poet Statius. Presented here (from K. M. Coleman's translation), the flowery passage was intended as public praise for the construction of a short extension of the Via Appia by his patron, the emperor Domitian (reigned 81–96).

> Here the first task is to start with the furrows, cut back the edges and hollow out the earth far down with deep excavation; next, to refill the scooped out trenches with other material and prepare a bed for the topmost camber [curved surface], so that the earth shall not wobble nor the spiteful ground provide a treacherous bed for the weight of [the paving] slabs; then to bind the road with blocks rammed in on both sides and numerous pegs. How many hands labor together! Some cut down groves and strip mountains, some smooth stakes and beams with iron; others bind together the slabs . . . [while] some dry up thirsty pools by hand and divert lesser streams far away.

firm enough both to support heavy traffic and to resist the damaging effects of weather for many years. Otherwise, the road's surface would eventually begin to settle, sag, sink, crack, and otherwise deteriorate. The depth of the trench the workers dug and the materials they used to refill it to make a firm bed varied from project to project and place to place. The chief variable was the nature of the soil and terrain at various points along the route, as Casson explains:

> Sometimes a road went over land so firm that there was no need whatsoever of a bed and all the gangs [of workers] had to do was level a track and place the paving stones right on the ground; there is a beautifully preserved stretch of the road that ran from Antioch to Chalcis in Syria laid this way. Where the ground was not that resistant the gangs trenched [i.e., dug trenches] until

they came to a firm enough layer. Into the trench they set
the bed, usually of more or less rounded stones in a mass
of clay or [claylike] earth; the thickness of the bed de-
pended entirely on how deep the trench had to go.
When a raised road was called for, as often happened,
the bed was built up until it overtopped the ground level
to the desired height. . . . Sometimes the surveyors simply could not avoid cutting across marshes or over sand,
and then the road gangs had to go to great lengths to
prepare a proper bed. One way was to open a deep
trench and simply toss in rock until so ponderous a load
of stone had been laid down that a firm bed resulted.
Where this would not work, they drove in wooden piers
[vertical supports], brought in the carpenters to fashion a
[horizontal] grillwork of wood [over the piers], and then
laid a gravel road over the wood.[12]

Surfaces and Other Features of Finished Roads
Having created a firm roadbed, which probably averaged two to
five feet in depth, the workers laid the surface of the road. Although that might, in some instances, consist of a layer of hard-
packed earth, gravel or paving stones were more durable and
therefore preferable. However, these two alternatives, especially paving stones, were also much more expensive. It must be
emphasized that few if any of the so-called paved Roman roads
had stone paving along their entire lengths. The great Via Appia itself was a case in point. The road's first stretch—from Rome
southward to the city of Capua, a distance of roughly 130
miles—was completed within a few years of its inauguration by
Appius Claudius in 312 B.C. In the following century, other road
builders extended the Via Appia southeastward across Italy to
the port of Brundisium, for an additional 240 miles or so. However, the road was originally surfaced with gravel. The first
paved section appears to have been a one-mile stretch located
within the city limits of Rome itself, completed in the 290s B.C.
Other sections of the Via Appia were paved at irregular intervals over the course of the next four centuries. And some scholars think that a few sections were never actually paved in stone,
but retained gravel or dirt surfaces.

Surfacing methods obviously varied with the materials. If
the builders chose to surface the road with gravel, they laid

down a thick layer of it and then compacted it by having men or animals drag huge stone rollers over it. If the choice was paving stones, they used one of two basic approaches. One was to cut the stones into rectangles, which abutted one another evenly at right angles; the Roman road that ran between the Near Eastern cities of Antioch and Aleppo was paved this way. The other method was to cut the stones into irregular polygons that fit together like the pieces of a jigsaw puzzle, a typical example being the paving stones of the Via Appia.

A section of the renowned Appian Way as it appears today.

Whether composed of gravel or stone, the surfaces of major Roman roads were cambered, that is, curved so that the middle was slightly higher than the sides. The intention was to make rainwater drain away from the road's surface. This not only kept water from pooling on the road, making it difficult or dangerous to use, but also greatly reduced the amount of water that might seep down through the gravel or stone and undermine the roadbed. Meanwhile, the unwanted water rolled harmlessly away into drainage ditches (*fossae*) dug by workers on either side of the road.

Finally, the better roads, especially in the sections near major cities, were outfitted with added amenities. In stretches where the road was steep, prone to being slippery, or otherwise dangerous, for instance, the builders carved artificial ruts into the surface (an idea borrowed from the Greeks and Etruscans). These tracks guided the wheels of carts and chariots, ensuring that these vehicles would not skid. Builders also placed high, flat-topped stones at intervals along the roadside so that travelers with horses could mount their steeds easier (since stirrups, taken for granted today, had not yet been invented). In his synopsis of the life of a second-century B.C. Roman politician and road builder named Gaius Gracchus, the first-century A.D.

Greek biographer Plutarch states: "He likewise placed other stones at small distances from one another, on both sides of the way, by the help of which travelers might get easily on horseback without wanting a groom."[13]

In addition, the road builders set up milestones (*miliaria*) at intervals of one Roman mile (which was about 285 feet shorter than a modern mile). Like modern road signs, these provided information about distances between towns and cities along the road. In time, other, more elaborate amenities sprang up alongside the major Roman highways to give aid and comfort to the many kinds of travelers who frequented these roads.

2

Life and Customs
Along the
Roman Roads

The major Roman roads were not simply bare conveniences to get from one place to another. As in the case of modern highways, various services and amenities—inns, eating places, stables, markets, chapels, and so on—were established along their routes; these outposts of civilization often developed into full-fledged villages and towns. In this way, travel along these roads became more inviting to even more people, who built still more roads, which stimulated the growth of more towns, and so forth, continuing the development of undeveloped regions. "Along these roads," Raymond Chevallier explains,

> posting stations and markets were set up, which, as time went by, developed into townships. Some remained one-street villages, others grew in size. The road often attracted the village. . . . We may understand what happened in the past . . . from the recent experience of newly developed lands. A road attracts people for a variety of reasons—sight-seeing, excitement, news and novelty, useful ideas and information, fashions and slogans, the variety of goods on offer. The fact that people could satisfy each other's needs and move easily around was the key to the many-sided development of town life. The initial grouping of population centered on the road was followed by a second phase in which there grew up a system of scattered settlements linked by short antennae to the main road.[14]

Moreover, as the major roads carried their services and amenities to distant parts of the Roman Empire, these microcosms

24

of Roman life and customs spread Roman civilization far and wide. The Roman influence had a unifying effect on the diverse lands and peoples who made up this huge realm. Like other leading Romans, the first-century A.D. Roman naturalist, Pliny the Elder, bragged of this achievement. Because "world-wide communications have been established thanks to the authority of the Roman Empire," he wrote with enthusiasm, "living standards [around the known world] have been improved by the interchange of goods and by partnership in the joy of peace and the general availability of [services and amenities] previously unknown to them."[15] Roman roads made this cultural unity possible, as soldiers, messengers, postmen, merchants, settlers, craftsmen, artists, poets, teachers, and tourists alike utilized them. Indeed, an examination of those who traveled the major roads and the services and culture that grew up along these routes reveals a veritable cross-section of ancient Roman life.

A nineteenth-century etching depicts an ancient Roman mail wagon, part of the famous government post set up by the first emperor, Augustus.

SOLDIERS AND COURIERS

Because the first large Roman highways were built primarily for strategic purposes, it is not surprising that the army made frequent use of them. Fast and easy movement of troops and officers was the most obvious such use. In his monumental *History of Rome from Its Foundation*, the first-century B.C. Roman historian Livy describes how, during a national emergency in the late third century B.C., the Roman dictator Fabius and his attendants "set out along the Flaminian Way [the Via Flaminia, a highway running northward from the capital] to meet the consul and his troops." Eventually, Fabius caught sight of "the consul riding towards him with his cavalry" along the road.[16] In another passage, Livy tells how, after a battle had been fought in the countryside, authorities in Rome sent "wagons and pack-animals" out on one of the major roads "to aid in the transport of men, exhausted as they were by fighting and by marching all night."[17] The army also used the road system for the swift dispatch of messengers. In the emergency mentioned above, Livy tells us, a Roman general "sent word in advance to the towns along the Appian Way . . . to have supplies ready within their own walls, and also to bring them down to the [main] road from the outlying farms [via the smaller roads]."[18]

Hannibal, the great Carthaginian general, took advantage of Rome's fine roads.

Unfortunately for the Romans, their extensive road system sometimes served their enemies. In the same emergency, the Carthaginian general Hannibal, who was attempting to subdue Italy, took advantage of its many fine roads to move his army through the countryside.

Government use of the roads was also nonmilitary. Like army generals in wartime, government officials dispatched messages along the road system. During Rome's republican years, this practice was irregular and the couriers were mostly slaves and freedmen (freed slaves). When Octavian (later renamed Augustus, the first Roman emperor) gained control of the Roman realm about 30 B.C., however, he set up a more regular and official system known as the *cursus publicus*, or "government post." As the service developed, his couriers were drawn mostly from the army, especially from units of highly skilled professional scouts (*speculatores*). For the most part, they traveled in horse-drawn carriages. Lionel Casson describes a relief (carving raised from a flat surface) found on the gravestone of one of these couriers:

> We see a *reda*, an open four-wheeled carriage, drawn by three horses, two in the yoke and a trace-horse. On the box [carriage frame] is a driver, who, plying the whip, keeps the team stepping smartly along. On a bench behind is the courier, wearing a hooded traveling cloak

AUGUSTUS ESTABLISHES THE GOVERNMENT POST

Here, from his *Lives of the Twelve Caesars*, the first-century A.D. Roman historian Suetonius describes the emperor Augustus's creation of the government post (*cursus publicus*).

> At the beginning of his reign he kept in close and immediate touch with provincial affairs by relays of runners strung out at short intervals along the highways; later, he organized a carriage service, based on posting stations—which has proved the more satisfactory arrangement, because post-boys can be cross-examined on the situation [in the place the message originated] as well as delivering written messages [so that it was better to have the same person take the message all the way]. The first seal Augustus used for safe-conducts, dispatches, and private letters was a sphinx [a mythical creature having the head of a woman and body of a lion]; next came a head of Alexander the Great [whom Augustus greatly admired]; lastly his own head . . . the seal which his successors continued to employ. He not only dated every letter, but entered the exact hour of the day or night when it was composed.

and holding what seems to be a riding crop. Behind him, facing rearward, is his servant, who sits on the baggage and clutches a lance with a distinctive head, a special insignia of office showing that his master was attached to the staff of the local governor.[19]

Couriers' travel ordinarily averaged about forty-five miles a day. But they could cover nearly three times that distance per day in an emergency.

To support the couriers, the *cursus publicus* maintained a network of facilities along the main roads. There were posting stations (*mutationes*), relay points where the carriage riders obtained fresh horses and perhaps a new wheel if one had been damaged, at regular intervals. Evidence suggests that the average interval was between seven thousand and twelve thousand paces. A Roman pace (the distance between a person's outstretched hands) was about five feet; thus the relay stations were about seven to twelve miles apart. There were also inns (*mansiones*) at regular intervals—usually between twenty and thirty miles—along the main roads, where the couriers, as well as other travelers, could stay overnight. The government did not build these inns; rather, it selected those that were conveniently placed along the route and ordered the owners to allow official couriers to stay for free. Thus, some of the financial burden for the upkeep of the government post fell on local communities and businesspeople.

Much later (in the early third century), the emperor Septimius Severus added another official transport service—the *cursus clabularis*. Its purpose was to carry provisions for the army overland using the main roads. Because this system required more people (administrators, handlers, drivers, and so on), large wagons and mule trains instead of carriages, and many more relay stations and inns, it was far more complex and expensive to operate than the government post.

TRADERS AND OTHER TRAVELERS

Merchants and traders used the road system, too, though rarely to carry bulky items long distances. This was because overland transport was very slow and consequently very expensive, and the heavier the items being transported, the higher the cost. Long-range trade was facilitated mainly by sailing ships, therefore. However, merchants did have to get some of their goods from the docks in port cities to inland villages and towns and from one inland town to another; where river transport was not practical, the roads carried this sort of trade.

The chief means of commercial land transport along Roman roads was the pack animal, most often the donkey or the mule. Horses were rarely used this way, partly because they were more expensive to raise and feed than donkeys or mules. (Of the latter, mules were generally preferable because they were stronger than donkeys; the maximum load of a donkey was about 250 pounds, and that of a mule about 450 pounds.) Mules were also generally superior to carts and wagons for transporting goods along the roads, although the use of such wheeled vehicles remained widespread. First, mules were cheaper, and second, they could easily travel along the many secondary country roads that were too narrow for large wagons. For very small loads, human carriers (porters) were also sometimes used. They commonly employed a wooden neck yoke that ran across their shoulders and held a large basket on each end.

Merchants and carriers who plied the roads regularly shared them with noncommercial travelers. The latter had any number of reasons for their journeys, from visiting relatives or friends, to tending to personal business, to attending religious festivals and

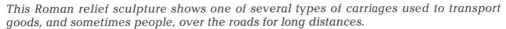

This Roman relief sculpture shows one of several types of carriages used to transport goods, and sometimes people, over the roads for long distances.

athletic events, to vacationing and sightseeing. Some rode in carriages or wagons. The few who could afford it lounged in litters, traveling couches equipped with pillows and canopies with draw curtains. For fairly short journeys, four to eight slaves bore a litter on their shoulders; for longer trips, the litter was most often attached to poles resting on the backs of mules. However, the majority of people using the roads probably walked, even on trips of hundreds of miles. (Though fine for shorter distances, horses were rarely used for long trips. This was partly because many travelers could not afford to own or rent a horse, and also because riding a horse for hours was highly uncomfortable, there being no stirrups and mere pieces of cloth for saddles.)

Because the travelers' pace was so slow, at least by modern standards, the longer journeys might take days, weeks, or on occasion even months. So they had to carry with them a considerable amount of clothing and baggage to meet daily as well as emergency needs. Casson provides this informative summary of what they customarily wore and carried:

> In addition to the inevitable kitchenware and tableware, towels, bedding, and the like, the traveler probably had to have more changes of clothing, as well as special wear adapted to the rigors of the road: heavy shoes or heavy sandals, broad-rimmed hat, and a selection of capes [for hot or cold days]. . . . Money and valuables were carried in a purse on a belt about the waist or in a little bag on a cord about the neck. Travelers who insisted on knowing the time could equip themselves with a pocket sundial. . . . Women on the road wore more or less the same clothes as men, though of greater length, reaching to the ankles. If they took along jewelry, they kept it out of sight.[20]

Among the other common items that travelers carried were food provisions, at least for lunches and snacks (they could get breakfast and supper at inns or restaurants); and gifts, either for those they planned to visit or for the owners of guesthouses where they intended to stay along the route. It was also very common for travelers to carry letters for various people, some of whom they did not know well or even at all. This informal postal system developed because the *cursus publicus* was reserved for government correspondence (although well-to-do and influential

WAGONS AND CARTS

In their *Handbook to Life in Ancient Rome*, English archaeologists Lesley Adkins and Roy A. Adkins give the following description of the wagons and other wheeled vehicles seen along Roman roads.

The design of [Roman] wheeled vehicles was borrowed from the Celts [the so-called barbarians who inhabited northern Europe], and nearly all the Latin names for vehicles were of Celtic . . . origin. . . . Passenger vehicles are more frequently portrayed in [Roman] art than commercial vehicles. The superstructure appears to have been light and flexible, at times made of wicker-work. No suspension was used, which must have made travel uncomfortable. For four-wheeled vehicles, it is uncertain if the Romans made use of a pivoting or a fixed axle, but the pivoting variety seems most likely. . . . Various types of wheel were used. The primitive solid wheel continued to be used . . . but spoked wheels were more common, and a number of

A mule- or horse-drawn wagon is depicted in this ancient Roman bas-relief.

complete wheels have been found. . . . These wheels usually had a single-piece iron tire, which was shrunk on, not nailed. . . . There is not much evidence for a braking system, but some means of keeping loaded vehicles under control on steep descents was necessary. A brake-pole dragging on the ground may have been used. Many roads were too narrow for two vehicles to pass, and it is possible that vehicles did not use the hard road surfaces except on bridges and in towns. Instead, it has been suggested that a dirt or grass verge alongside the paved road was used.

individuals no doubt managed fairly often to get their personal letters into official pouches), and there was no public postal service, as is practically universal today. So the majority of people, who could not afford their own private couriers (another way wealthy people got their mail delivered), had to rely on travelers. The usual procedure was to find someone who was headed to or near the destination of the letter's recipient.

HORACE'S JOURNEY TO BRUNDISIUM

Depending on what he or she could afford, a traveler carried most of this diverse baggage in carts, on mules, on the backs of porters, on his or her own back, or in some combination of these. But alas, having plenty of necessities and other baggage within easy reach did not guarantee a pleasant or comfortable trip. Whether one

The great Roman poet Horace and his companions traversed this very stretch of the famed Via Appia on their way to the southern Italian city of Brundisium.

A TRAVELER PAYS HIS BILL

The following inscription (quoted in Jo-Ann Shelton's *As the Romans Did*), which depicts a traveler paying his bill at an inn, gives a general idea of the services offered by such establishments.

"Innkeeper, my bill please!"

"You had one *sextarius* [pint] of wine, one *as* [a common bronze coin] worth of bread, two *asses* worth of relishes."

"That's right."

"You had a girl [i.e., a prostitute] for eight *asses*."

"Yes, that's right."

"And two *asses* worth of hay for your mule."

"That damned mule will ruin me yet."

walked or rode, long trips on Roman roads were at best arduous and sometimes miserable. In one of his satires, the famous first-century B.C. Roman poet Horace left behind a fascinating description of an uncomfortable trip he took from Rome to Brundisium on the equally famous Appian Way. The journey of roughly 370 miles took several days. Along the way Horace experienced "greedy innkeepers," "foul water" that made him sick to his stomach, and mosquitoes and croaking frogs that "made sleep impossible." Although he and his fellow travelers (including the renowned epic poet Virgil) had a very comfortable overnight stay at the villa of a wealthy friend, the rest of the trip was almost as tiring and unpleasant as the beginning. "From Caudium we headed directly toward Beneventum," he writes,

> where the overly eager innkeeper almost burned down his whole place while roasting some scrawny thrushes on a spit. . . . Had you been there, you would have seen hungry guests and frightened slaves grabbing the food, and everyone trying to put out the fire. Soon after Beneventum, Apulia began to reveal her mountains, so familiar to me. They

were scorched by the hot wind, and we would never have managed to crawl through them if an inn near Trivicum had not taken us in for the night. But it was filled with eye-stinging smoke because there were damp branches, leaves and all, burning in the fireplace. . . . When we finally reached Rubi, we were exhausted . . . and the trip was made even more uncomfortable by rain. The weather improved the next day, but the road was worse. . . . Finally [we made it to] Brundisium, the end of a long trip.[21]

LODGING AND FOOD

Notable in Horace's narrative are his frequent mentions of the lodgings in which he and his fellow travelers stayed. By the second century A.D. the vast network of roads traversing the Roman Empire, from present-day Spain and France in the west to Egypt and Syria in the east, were dotted by thousands of inns. Some were built in existing towns that happened to be near major highways; others sprang up along open stretches of road. The latter frequently went on to become the nuclei of new towns, as the names of some Roman and later European towns attest. The town of Tres Tabernae, situated along the Appian Way south of Rome, for example, means literally "three inns" (the word *taberna*, from which the modern word *tavern* comes, was a common Latin word for inn; it could also mean a shop or a hut). The modern French towns of Saverne, Tavers, Tavernieres, and Tavernolles are all derived from the same word; these and hundreds of other modern settlements owe their existence to the fine road system that once crisscrossed the Roman world.

The names of the inns themselves were varied and often colorful. Animal names were popular (the Camel, the Elephant). So were the names of gods (the Mercury and Apollo, the Diana) and of everyday tools, weapons, and other objects (the Wheel, the Sword). Whatever they might be called, they all offered the same basic services, namely food, lodging for the night, and a change of wagons or pack animals. The layout and look of an average Roman roadside inn is known, thanks to the work of archaeologists (scholars who excavate and study the remains of past cultures). One such inn, excavated in what is now Austria, was a two-story structure about seventy feet long and forty feet wide. A court for wagons and carriages ran

This street in Saverne, France, decorated for Christmas, was originally a Roman road, around which the town grew up and expanded over many centuries.

along one side and the ground floor had a stable that could accommodate perhaps a dozen animals. It also featured a blacksmith's forge, a large kitchen, a dining room (which was equipped with heating ducts under the floor), and several bedrooms on the second story.

Some roadside country inns were larger and more elaborate, but they still offered the same basic services, as did the inns in the towns located along or near the major roads. There were certain advantages to staying in a town, however, as opposed to an isolated country inn. For example, all Roman towns of at least moderate size had public baths, many of which featured not only hot and cold pools in which to relax, but also snack bars, exercise and massage rooms, and even libraries and reading rooms. Towns also offered several different kinds of eating places, from simple snack bars that sold

Roman bathhouses, like this one in Bath, England, were often large, complex structures featuring exercise rooms, snack bars, and other amenities.

fast food to more elegant establishments with multiple dining rooms. In the town of Pompeii (near modern Naples), the main street alone featured twenty restaurants (one every thirty yards or so).

Whether in town or along open stretches of road, travelers who could not afford or for some reason did not want to stay at inns could avail themselves of private lodgings. As remains common today in many parts of the world, owners of private houses rented out rooms, which were as a rule less expensive than the ones at the inns. Not much is known about specific Roman guesthouses, but a rather humorous inscription on a plaque that hung outside one of these houses has survived. "If you're clean and neat," it reads, "then there's a house ready and waiting for you. If you're dirty—well, I'm ashamed to say it, but you're welcome too."[22]

ROAD BOOKS AND MAPS

Ancient travelers on the Roman roads, especially those going long distances, needed to know where these thousands of inns, guesthouses, and other facilities were located. So they bought pamphletlike road books called *itineraria* (from which the modern word *itinerary*, meaning a list of scheduled destinations, is derived). Each of these road books listed the towns, inns, stables, major sites, and other notable places along a given road or route (which might be a combination of many different roads, as in the case of the route from Rome to a major town in Spain).

A few such road books have survived. One, created in the early fourth century, when Christianity was rising to prominence in the Roman Empire, was apparently intended for use by religious pilgrims; it shows the route from Burdigala (modern Bordeaux), in Gaul, to Jerusalem, in Palestine (the Holy Land). The portion of the itinerary within Gaul lists roads totaling about 370 miles and identifies thirty posting stations and eleven inns. Also listed are numerous short unspecified detours along the way, which may have been to visit local chapels or the guesthouses of fellow Christians.

Also available were road maps that were quite similar in some ways to modern road guides. One of these has survived, in a fashion. A medieval copy of an ancient Roman map, this priceless relic, called the Peutinger Table, was discovered in Germany in the late fifteenth century and now rests in the Library of Vienna, in Austria. The map, measuring thirteen inches wide by twenty-two feet long, shows the lands composing the Roman Empire and the road systems within each. The names of towns and cities are shown, as are numbers indicating the distances between them in Roman miles.

The map has, in addition, little symbols representing inns, posting stations, and other stopping places, categorized by the extent and quality of the facilities offered, just as in modern guides. One symbol, for example, is a picture of a four-sided building with a courtyard in the middle; apparently it stands for an inn with excellent facilities. A symbol of a house with a twin-peaked roof, on the other hand, stands for a country inn of average means; a house with a single-peaked roof means a very modest inn; and so forth. (It is important to emphasize that the Peutinger Table is not drawn to scale, as modern maps are. Instead, it is purposely representational, meant simply to indicate which roads and facilities existed in a given area and the number of miles from one road intersection and facility to another.)

LURKING DANGERS

Unfortunately, Roman road books and maps could not pinpoint the dangers that lurked along the roads, which travelers tried to avoid but ran into from time to time. In his *Golden Ass*, the second-century A.D. Roman writer Apuleius describes a fairly typical example of highway robbery. "You will remember that I made for Macedonia on a business trip," says the victim:

> I was . . . making my way home with a good bit of money in my pocket. Shortly before reaching Larissa [in Greece] . . . I was making my way along a . . . valley when I was held up by some brigands of massive physique who robbed me of all my money.[23]

ATTACKS BY HUNGRY WOLVES

In his work *The Golden Ass*, the second-century A.D. Roman novelist Apuleius includes the following passage dramatizing (and probably exaggerating) the danger that wolves posed to travelers on some roads.

> As evening overshadowed our path, we came to a crowded and prosperous village. The inhabitants there tried to deter us from leaving in darkness or even in early morning. They said that there were hordes of gigantic wolves plaguing all that district; they were burly and big-bodied, exceedingly fierce and savage, and were constantly hunting plunder [victims] in many areas. . . . Like highwaymen [robbers] they attacked travelers as they passed by. Indeed, their mad hunger made them so savage that they stormed neighboring farmhouses, and the fate suffered by unresisting cattle now overhung the human occupants themselves. They claimed that the road on which we were to travel was littered with half-devoured bodies, all gleaming white because the bones had been stripped of their flesh. Hence it was vital that we observe the greatest caution in resuming our journey, and take the most stringent care to travel in broad daylight . . . [and] proceed not strung out in isolation, but in compact wedge-formation.

A hair-raising example of a roadside robbery is reported in a third-century A.D. letter written to a friend by one Psois, a resident of the Roman province of Egypt: "Just as we were rejoicing at being about to arrive home, we fell into an attack by bandits . . . and some of us were killed. . . . Thank god I escaped with just being stripped clean."[24] Both narrators were lucky that they escaped unhurt; as the second testifies, some less fortunate travelers lost their lives along with their money.

Other dangers awaited the unwary on the highways. One common sort consisted of run-ins with soldiers, who, either singly or in small groups, sometimes took advantage of hapless civilians. In his book, for instance, Apuleius includes an episode in which a well-armed soldier bearing a message to Rome seizes a donkey from an unarmed man. Apuleius also describes the danger posed to travelers by wolves and farm dogs. In one passage, the inhabitants of a village warn some travelers about "hordes of gigantic wolves" plaguing the area. They advise traveling

Soldiers like this one sometimes harassed civilians along the roads.

only in daylight and "not strung out in isolation, but in compact wedge-formation."[25] Though Apuleius likely exaggerated this danger for dramatic effect, wolves no doubt prowled some of the more isolated areas through which the roads passed. In another passage from Apuleius's work, some farmers, thinking the travelers are robbers, sic their guard dogs on them:

> These animals were wild, huge, and . . . ferocious. . . . Their native savagery was intensified by the din [racket] their masters made. They charged at us, surrounded us on all sides, and leapt at us from every angle. . . . Their sustained attacks left many of us lying on the ground.[26]

There is no way to know how often travelers encountered thieves, errant soldiers, dangerous animals, and other perils along the roadways. But most people must have judged that the benefits outweighed the risks, for Rome's road system remained heavily traveled throughout Rome's tenure as master of the Mediterranean world.

3

BUILDING THE ROMAN AQUEDUCTS

Like people in all times and places, the Romans required supplies of fresh water. To meet this need they built their now world-famous system of aqueducts, channels that conveyed large quantities of water to major towns and cities. They did not always have aqueducts, of course; the first one, the Aqua Appia, which served the capital city, was not erected until 312 B.C. (by Appius Claudius, who also built the first major road, the Via Appia). Moreover, even when most of the Roman aqueducts were in place (roughly by the late second century A.D.), many towns and most villages still drew their water by other, more traditional means.

WHY AQUEDUCTS WERE MORE PRACTICAL

As might be expected, the earliest water sources the Romans exploited were streams, rivers, and wells, which continued to be used in many areas throughout the years of the Republic and Empire. Sometime in the sixth century B.C. these sources began to be supplemented by cisterns, artificial reservoirs for collecting and storing rainwater. The Romans usually placed them on rooftops, although they sometimes set them up at ground level. A variation that appeared in the early third century B.C. was the *compluvium/impluvium*, a simple but useful system that was most often installed in a house's foyer or central hall, called an *atrium* (kitchens being another common location). The *compluvium* was a rectangular opening in the roof and the *impluvium* a shallow basin situated directly below it; when it rained, water flowed across the roof (which was slanted slightly toward the middle), through the opening, and down into the basin. Public buildings, especially bathhouses, had cisterns too, usually a good deal larger than the domestic variety.

All of these nonaqueduct methods of gathering water had the same basic disadvantages. First, Jean-Pierre Adam explains, the water they provided "had to be drawn. This had then to be carried, manually or with raising devices, to the place of use, or diverted into raised reservoirs in order to be then distributed under pressure." By contrast, he continues,

> the creation of aqueducts fed by permanent springs made it possible to resolve all the problems of water catchment, transport, reliability of supply and distribution to all parts of the city or to a system of agricultural irrigation.[27]

For these reasons, as the populations of Rome and other cities in its dominion increased and demand for fresh water grew apace, the Romans began building aqueducts.

As in the case of road systems and the government post, the Romans did not invent the concept of the aqueduct. A seventh-century B.C. Babylonian king named Sennacherib constructed an aqueduct of stone blocks, mortar, and concrete to carry water from a canal to his capital city, Nineveh. And the Greeks built aqueducts too. Perhaps the most famous, created in the sixth century B.C. on the Aegean island of Samos, ran for more than a half-mile through the center of a small mountain.

But what the Romans lacked in originality, they amply made up for in determination, daring, ingenuity, and sheer energy. In time, their system of aqueducts and water distribution far surpassed any that had come before. The city of Rome was eventually supplied by eleven aqueducts and there were numerous others in Italy, Gaul,

The Assyrian king and noted aqueduct-builder, Sennacherib.

Spain, Greece, and other parts of the realm. The capital city's eleven aqueducts alone ran for a total of more than 260 miles.

The remains of this bridge section of a Roman aqueduct, located north of Madrid, Spain, are in an excellent state of preservation.

(It should be noted that only thirty miles, or about one-ninth, of this distance featured tall rows of stone arches, called arcades. These structures, which were essentially bridges erected to carry the water channels through certain areas, are sometimes confused with the channels themselves, which were the actual aqueducts.) With good reason, the Romans were very proud of this unique engineering accomplishment. Sextus Julius Frontinus, who served as water commissioner for the capital city in the late first century A.D., expressed this pride, boasting, "With such an array of indispensable structures carrying so many waters, compare, if you will, the idle [Egyptian] Pyramids or the useless, though famous, works of the Greeks!"[28]

FINDING AND TESTING WATER SOURCES

When completed, a Roman aqueduct was an extensive, complex, and masterfully crafted combination of conduits, tunnels, bridges, pools, reservoirs, pipes, and nozzles. But even before the planning stages of such a project, it was first necessary to find a plentiful and reliable water source. In some areas this was a relatively easy task. The inland region near the city of Rome (bordering the plain of Latium in the north), for instance, has many hills and small mountains. Rain and melting snow from these elevated locations flow downward; some of the water feeds rivers, such as the famous Tiber, which flows by Rome, and the rest sinks into the ground and emerges in various places as springs. The Romans correctly

FRONTINUS, A DILIGENT PUBLIC SERVANT

Sextus Julius Frontinus (ca. A.D. 30–ca. 104) was a noted Roman public official and writer. He served as governor of the province of Britain, where he distinguished himself as a military leader, and in 97 the emperor Nerva appointed him water commissioner (*curator aquarum*) of Rome. It was during this diligent service that Frontinus composed his best-known work, *The Aqueducts of Rome*. Modern historians find the book very valuable for its detailed histories and lists of physical specifications for all of the capital city's aqueducts. In his introduction, he states the purpose and plan of the book.

> Inasmuch as every task assigned by the emperor demands special attention; and inasmuch as . . . Nerva Augustus . . . has laid upon me the duties of water commissioner . . . I deem it of the first and greatest importance to familiarize myself with the business I have undertaken. . . . Observing, therefore, the practice I have followed in many offices, I have gathered in this sketch . . . such facts, hitherto [before this] scattered, as I have been able to get together, which bear on the general subject. . . . I will first set down the names of the waters which enter the City of Rome; then I will tell by whom . . . and in what year . . . each one was brought in . . . how far each is carried in a subterranean channel, how far on substructures, [and] how far on arches. Then I will give . . . how many public reservoirs there are, and from these how much [water] is delivered to public works, how much to . . . fountains [and so forth].

saw that, if properly tapped and exploited, these springs had the potential to supply the capital city with all the fresh water it needed.

In contrast, in drier, less hilly regions, where springs were few or nonexistent, finding water was not always easy. Over time, the Romans, like other peoples before them, developed ways of finding water that did not flow or pool directly on the earth's surface. The first-century B.C. Roman architect Vitruvius, whose informative book on engineering survives, gives the following recommendations:

> Water will be more accessible if the springs flow in the open. But if they do not flow above ground, sources are to be sought and collected underground. The method of trial is to fall on one's face before sunrise in the place

The Romans originally obtained their water for drinking, cooking, and irrigation from the Tiber River, shown here flowing through Rome today.

where the search is to take place, and placing and supporting one's chin on the ground, to look round the neighborhood. . . . Digging is to be carried out where moisture seems to curl upwards and rise into the air; for this indication cannot arise on dry ground. . . . The following [plant] growths will be found to show where the kinds of soil [having fresh water beneath them] are found: the slender bulrush, the wild willow, the alder . . . reeds, ivy, and the like which cannot grow without [considerable] moisture. These plants usually grow in marshy places. . . . When such a discovery is indicated, we must make trials in the following way. A hole is to be dug not less than three feet square and five feet deep, and about sunset a bronze or lead vessel, or a basin, is to be placed there. . . . On the next day it is to be opened, and if there are drops of water and moisture in the vessel, water will be found.[29]

Of course, not all water sources were equally clean and usable. That is one reason why river water, which tended to be filled with sediment, was avoided if cleaner sources could be found. In an age when chemical treatment and purification of water had not yet been invented, the Romans had to be careful to choose the cleanest, purest sources possible; therefore, they developed ways to test for purity. According to Vitruvius:

If a fresh spring be dug, and the water, being sprinkled over a vessel of . . . good bronze, leave no trace [of residue], the water is very good. Or if water is boiled in a copper vessel and is allowed to stand and then poured off, it will also pass the test, if no sand or mud is found in the bottom. . . . [And] if vegetables being put in the vessel with water and boiled, are soon [i.e., rapidly] cooked, they will show that the water is good and wholesome.[30]

CHOOSING THE BEST ROUTE

Having found an abundant and clean water source, the builders could begin construction of the aqueduct. It is difficult for modern scholars to know and describe exactly how such structures were originally built, for two reasons. First, outside of Frontinus's and Vitruvius's books, the Greeks and Romans wrote almost nothing about aqueducts (at least nothing that has survived), and neither of these writers says much about their actual construction. Second, aqueducts were repaired and overhauled so often over the centuries that a major portion of the original work has been erased. Still, enough evidence has survived to piece together a fairly clear idea of the step-by-step process of erecting a Roman aqueduct.

It is clear, for example, that aqueduct builders themselves faced some major difficulties and challenges in the initial stages of a project. As in the case of roads, surveyors first had to lay out a route; but unlike a roadbed, which was kept straight and direct whenever possible, an aqueduct's route was often purposely indirect, with several twists and turns. This design was necessary because an aqueduct moved water by exploiting the natural force of gravity rather than by placing it under pressure, the method that is more common today. The aqueduct's water channel, called the *specus*, was very slightly inclined, or slanted downward from the horizontal, just enough to induce the water to flow downward from its source. The amount of the incline varied somewhat from place to place, but averaged about two to three feet per mile; in other words, the water flowed from point A to point B because point B was slightly lower in elevation than point A. Therefore, the builders laid the *specus* along whatever route most efficiently maintained the desired incline, even if doing so meant zigzagging through the countryside. Adam elaborates:

> The great length of some aqueducts was due not only to the distance from the water catchment, but also to the lie of the land. Obstacles had to be crossed or bypassed without imposing too many constraints on the average incline to be maintained. In fact, it was preferable to avoid level stretches [the preferred areas for roads] which caused the water to stagnate, but equally too strong [steep] an incline brought about the rapid erosion of the watertight lining of the channel. To break the speed of a strong current of water on a long incline, the engineers were sometimes forced to create short falls . . . between two reservoirs, making it possible then to resume a slight and regular incline.[31]

With these considerations in mind, the surveyors first determined the differences in elevation among the hills, plains, and other natural features between the water source and the target

THE LASTING IMPACT OF VITRUVIUS'S WORK

Marcus Vitruvius Pollio was a practicing Roman architect from about 46 to 30 B.C. Beyond this, very little is known about his life. He was apparently already an old man by the late 20s B.C., when he penned the ten books composing his great treatise—*On Architecture*. In the preface of the work, he explained that it was dedicated to his mentor, the emperor Augustus:

> I set about the composition of this work for you. For I perceived that you have built, and are now building, on a large scale. Furthermore, with respect to the future, you have such regard to public and private buildings, that they will correspond to the grandeur of our history, and will be a memorial to future ages. . . . In the following books, I have expounded a complete system of architecture.

This illustration was drawn for a later European edition of Vitruvius's book.

The last sentence was no idle boast, for the work covers all types of Greek and Roman building, as well as methods of decoration, mathematics, and diverse aspects of civil engineering, including aqueducts and water distribution. Vitruvius's service to Augustus turned out to have lasting impact. After Rome's fall, *On Architecture* survived in various medieval handwritten copies. The edition published in 1486 became a sudden sensation among European architects and established the neoclassical building style that dominated Europe for centuries and even influenced American architects such as Thomas Jefferson.

city. To accomplish this, they used an instrument called a *dioptra*, topped by a horizontal disk in which a small channel was inlaid. The surveyor filled the channel with water and tilted the disk until the water level was even with the surface of the disk, which told him that the instrument itself was level. Then he

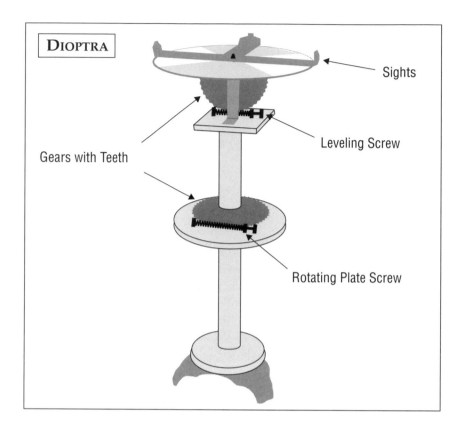

peered through a sight mounted on the disk's edge, focusing on his assistant, who stood in the distance holding a staff in a vertical position. By lining up the top surface of the *dioptra* with markers attached to the distant staff and doing some mathematical calculations, the surveyor could tell how much higher or lower the ground was where the assistant was standing. This sounds reasonably simple. But the instrument was not very accurate unless its sighting distance was rather short, which meant that it had to be set up hundreds of times over the course of a typical proposed route. Once this laborious task had been completed, the surveyor could calculate the route that best maintained the desired incline; accordingly, he then marked that route with wooden posts.

DIGGING THE BED FOR THE WATER CHANNEL

Finally, it was time for gangs of workers to begin clearing the land along the route, as well as digging trenches and tunnels and building arcades wherever required. Apparently, these laborers were mostly hired freemen who lived in the towns along the route, as was the case with the workers on the crews that built roads; however, the more backbreaking and dangerous

TWO TUNNELS INSTEAD OF ONE?

One of the few surviving ancient documents relating to the construction of aqueducts is the following report (quoted in Ivor Hart's *The Great Engineers*) filed by the Roman engineer Nonius Datus in A.D. 152. While an aqueduct he had designed was under construction near Saldae, in North Africa, he made the mistake of leaving to tend to other business; he returned to find that the workmen had botched the construction of a tunnel.

> I found everybody sad and despondent. They had given up all hopes that the opposite sections of the tunnel would meet, because each section had already been excavated beyond the middle of the mountain. As always happens in these cases, the fault was attributed to me, the engineer, as though I had not taken all precautions to ensure the success of the work. What could I have done better? For I began by surveying and taking the levels of the mountain, I drew plans and sections of the whole work. . . . And to take extra precaution, I summoned the contractor and his workmen and began the excavation in their presence with the help of two gangs of experienced veterans. . . . What more could I have done? After four years' absence, expecting every day to hear the good tidings of the water at Saldae, I arrived. The contractor and his assistants had made blunder upon blunder. In each section of the tunnel they had diverged from the [straight] line, each towards the right, and had I waited a little longer before coming, Saldae would have possessed two tunnels instead of one!

Luckily, Datus set to work with a new crew of workers and, with some considerable effort, was able to correct the mistake.

jobs, especially tunneling, were probably given to slaves. Also, in the case of the aqueducts serving the capital city, some of the workers were undoubtedly unemployed urban dwellers who trekked out to the work camps for the chance of some welcome, if temporary, employment.

Day after day, the workers dug and shaped the bed in which the *specus* would be constructed along most of the aqueduct's length. (The aboveground arcades would account for only a small fraction of the distance, mostly on the final approach to the city.) The easiest stretches were obviously those where the ground was soft and shovels could be used. The men used pieces of timber to shore up the sides of the trenches until the blocks of stone that would make up the channel could be hauled to the work site and prepared by stonemasons. When the route passed over rocky areas, the trench had to be dug mostly with picks and hammers; even more difficult was tunneling through hills and other solid obstructions along the route. Those unfortunates assigned to this task, the Hameys write,

> had first to sink a *puteus*, a shaft, every seventy-one meters (233 feet) or so; then, with just enough room for one man to work at the rock face, they would tunnel forward, passing back the hewn stone in baskets to be hauled up the shaft. Without free-flowing air, the atmosphere [in the shaft] would soon become foul from the oil-lamps and the breathing of the workmen.[32]

Occasionally, an aqueduct tunnel was so long that it became very difficult to ensure that both ends would meet at the right spot in the middle. (Shafts were excavated simultaneously from opposite sides to make sure that the tunnel started and ended precisely in alignment with the designated route.) In A.D. 152, while digging such a tunnel for an aqueduct under construction in what is now Algeria (then part of one of Rome's north African provinces), the two teams of tunnelers missed each other by several feet. The engineer in charge of the project complained:

> As always happens in these cases, the fault was attributed to me, the engineer, as though I had not taken all precautions to ensure the success of the work. . . . The contractor and his assistants had made blunder upon

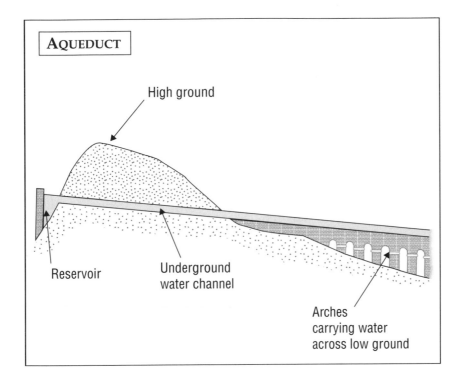

AQUEDUCT

High ground

Reservoir

Underground
water channel

Arches
carrying water
across low ground

blunder. In each section of the tunnel they had diverged
from the [straight] line, each towards the right.[33]

While the workers were digging the bed for the water channel, it was of the utmost importance that the floor of the bed main-
tain the desired downward slope; otherwise, after the channel
was laid in the bed the water would flow too fast or not at all. So
the on-site engineer (or surveyor) frequently measured the
amount of incline at the bottom of the bed to make sure specifications were being met. He did this by lowering into the bed an instrument known as a *chorobates*, which Vitruvius described as

> a straight plank about twenty feet long. At the extreme
> ends it has legs made to correspond [with each other],
> and fastened at right angles to the ends of the plank, and,
> between the plank and the legs, cross-pieces joined by
> tenons [wooden joints]. These have lines accurately
> drawn to a perpendicular [vertical line], and plummets
> [plumb bobs, or small metal weights] hanging . . . over
> the lines from the plank. When the plank is in position,

the perpendiculars which touch equally and of like measure the lines marked, indicate the level position of the instrument.[34]

Once the *chorobates* was in place in the bed, the engineer checked to see if the plumb lines hung in the desired positions. If they did not, he slipped chocks (wooden wedges) under one end until they hung correctly and then ordered the workmen to make the floor of the bed conform to the incline indicated.

Laying the Channel

When the engineer was satisfied that the bed had been dug correctly and that the incline was right, he gave the go-ahead for laying in the *specus*, the heart of the aqueduct. This channel was made of stone blocks that measured twenty by fifty inches on average and was usually about as high and wide as an average doorway. To keep the channel watertight and clean, the inside was coated with a special mortar mixed with small pieces of broken tile to give it extra strength. When the mortar was dry, the workmen lowered the top stones into place, sealing the aqueduct. They then buried it, so that it remained underground, except in the short stretches (across ravines, for example) where it emerged to run atop arcades.

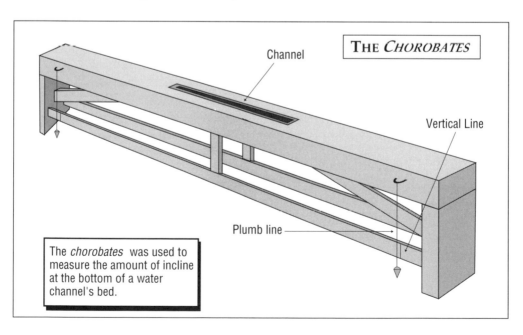

The *chorobates*

Channel

Vertical Line

Plumb line

The *chorobates* was used to measure the amount of incline at the bottom of a water channel's bed.

The milestones used for Roman aqueducts in many ways resembled this road milestone, erected under the emperor Macrinus in about A.D. 218.

In the era during which the Romans built their first aqueducts, they had not yet conquered all of Italy, and enemy armies still occasionally threatened the region of their capital city. So for a long time they did not mark the locations of the buried aqueducts, for fear that an enemy might find them and destroy their life-giving water supply. Later, however, after Rome had come to dominate not only Italy but many lands beyond it, this was no longer a worry and aqueduct builders began installing milestones, called *cippi*, along the route. This made locating specific sections of the aqueducts much easier when repairs were needed, which turned out to be often. Indeed, maintaining the aqueducts and their water distribution systems turned out to be almost as big a job as building these structures in the first place.

WATER DISTRIBUTION AND AQUEDUCT MAINTENANCE

By A.D. 206, the city of Rome, hub of an empire that encompassed all the lands bordering the shores of the Mediterranean Sea, was supplied by eleven aqueducts. Among these were the Aqua Appia (initiated in 312 B.C.), the first to be built; the Aqua Anio (272 B.C.), later called the Anio Vetus, or "Old Anio," to distinguish it from one with the same name built later (the Anio Novus, or "New Anio," A.D. 38); the Aqua Marcia (144 B.C.), at 58.4 miles the longest of the eleven; and the Aqua Claudia (A.D. 38), today the best preserved of the eleven.

The remains of part of the Aqua Claudia, the best preserved of Rome's eleven aqueducts.

The daily output of (number of gallons supplied by) each of these aqueducts varied, as do modern estimates for these outputs, but a reasonable guess for the total output of the eleven combined is 250 million gallons a day. Since the city of Rome had roughly one million inhabitants in the early third century, that yields about 250 gallons of water per person per day. In comparison, the water department of the average American town supplies about 125 gallons per person per day.

This enormous volume of water flowing into ancient Rome began at the springs and other sources in the hills, what can be thought of as the "back" end of the aqueducts. It then traveled through the countryside within the various water channels until it reached the city. There, on what can be thought of as the "front" end of the aqueducts, the flow entered a complex distribution system that carried the water to fountains, public baths, houses, and so on. (Like the extensive stretches of water channels buried in the countryside, the distribution portion of the system was largely and conveniently hidden from view.) Considering how large and complicated the aqueduct system was, as well as the great amount of wear and tear it had to withstand, it is hardly surprising that maintenance and repair was a constant and enormous task. This prompted the creation of Rome's water commission, of which Frontinus was the director (*curator aquarum*) in the late first century. Thanks to him and his book, modern scholars know a fair amount about this aspect of the Roman aqueducts.

FILTERING THE WATER

The most vital point in the front end of an aqueduct was the main distribution building (*castellum aquae*). It was located near

Pompeii's castellum aquae, *pictured here, is extraordinarily well preserved because it was encased in volcanic ash by the* A.D. *79 eruption of Mt. Vesuvius.*

the outer edge of the town being supplied, usually on the highest elevation in the area so that water would flow downward from this structure into the town. Having run for miles through the countryside, the *specus* entered the distribution building, where the water flowed into a large reservoir or holding tank.

The reservoir had two purposes. First, it cleaned the water, which, even if it had come from a mountain spring, was apt to contain some sediment or other impurities. There were two purification methods, usually used in conjunction. The first consisted of metal grills (screens with very small holes), one set up where the *specus* entered the building and one or more inside. These filtered out the larger particles. The other filtering device was settling tanks (*piscinae limariae*), in which the water was allowed to sit for a while so that impurities would slowly settle to the bottom. (Workers periodically emptied these tanks and cleaned them.) Examples of these apparatuses have survived in various places around the Mediterranean world, some of the best preserved being those in the *castellum aquae* at Pompeii. This building, as Jean-Pierre Adam describes it,

> was built to the north of the city near the "Vesuvius Gate," at the highest point of the city, i.e., 34m (about 111 feet) above the lowest point at the south, the Stabian Gate, just 750m (about 2,460 feet) away. . . . The building, of trapezoidal shape, encloses a circular domed chamber, 5.7m (about 19 feet) in diameter and 4.3m (about 14.2 feet) high, into which the *specus* of the aqueduct flowed. The water passed through a grill on entering the settling tank, which was bordered on each side by a service walkway. A second grill, probably a finer one, went across the middle of the basin.[35]

THE USE OF WATER PIPES

The other purpose of the reservoir within the distribution building was, exactly as the bulding's name suggests, to distribute, or spread out and deliver, the aqueduct's purified water to various points in the town. This was accomplished using pipes. Many people today are surprised to learn that the Romans were quite adept at making pipes, which were fashioned from bronze, wood, ceramic tile, concrete, and lead. Each of these materials had certain advantages and disadvantages for pipe making. As noted scholar L. Sprague de Camp explains:

Bronze makes a fine strong pipe, but is hard to work and costly, so that sections left unguarded were liable to be stolen. Wood rots and splits; while tile and concrete, though durable, have but little strength in tension and so cannot withstand much pressure from inside.[36]

As for using lead to make water pipes, on the positive side it is very durable and can withstand considerable pressure. It is also very malleable (flexible), so that it can be bent into any shape desired, making it ideal for water pipes, which often need to wind over, under, or around various existing obstacles. On the negative side, lead, like bronze, was very expensive in ancient times. This was partly because mining and transporting lead was difficult and also because preparing it and shaping it into pipes required workmen with special skills. They constructed such pipes by warming the metal until it was soft, rolling it into thin sheets, wrapping these around cylindrical wooden templates (forms), and soldering (seal-

This surviving section of a Roman lead water pipe still bears the inscription etched by its makers.

ing) the seams with liquid lead. Two lengths of pipe were joined together by wrapping a metal collar around the junction and soldering its edges shut with lead.

Another shortcoming of lead for use in making water pipes is that consumption of this metal is dangerous to human health. And at least some Romans were well aware of this problem. According to Vitruvius, water

seems to be made injurious by lead, because white lead [used to make paint] is produced by it; and this is said to be harmful to the human body. . . . We can take example from the workers in lead who have complexions affected by pal-lor [paleness]. For when, in casting, the lead receives the current of air, the fumes from it occupy the members [parts] of the body, and burning them thereupon, rob the limbs of

THE AQUA CLAUDIA: ONE OF THE WONDERS OF THE WORLD

In this section of his *Natural History* (John Healy's translation), the first-century Roman encyclopedist Pliny the Elder praises the Aqua Claudia, begun by the emperor Caligula (Gaius Caesar) in A.D. 38 and finished by the emperor Claudius in 52.

Let us now move on to achievements which are unsurpassed because of their real value. The most recent and costly project, begun by the emperor Gaius and completed by Claudius, has surpassed all previous aqueducts. The springs called Curtius and Caeruleus, as well as the Anio Novus, were made to flow into Rome from the fortieth milestone at such a high level as to provide water for all the hills of the city; the work cost 350 million sesterces [*sestertii*]. If we ponder the abundant water supply in public buildings, baths, open channels, private houses, gardens, and country estates; if we consider the distances traveled by the water, the building of the arches, the tunneling through mountains, and the construction of level routes across valleys; we can only conclude that this is a supreme wonder of the world.

This recent photo shows one of the Aqua Claudia's several well-preserved sections of arcade.

the virtues of the blood. Therefore it seems that water should not be brought in lead pipes if we desire to have it wholesome.[37]

Unfortunately, this and other occasional ancient warnings about the dangers of lead were ignored (and eventually forgotten, for lead poisoning was not properly diagnosed until the 1700s). And the Romans continued to use lead extensively for water pipes.

Eventually, many of the lead pipes installed in Roman water systems were replaced by ceramic ones. But this was in response to lead's rising costs, not its potential harmful properties. Vitruvius himself recommends the use of ceramics (or earthenware) as a way to save money:

> If we wish to employ a less expensive method [of making pipes], we must proceed as follows. Earthenware pipes are to be made not less than two inches thick, and so tongued that they may enter into and fit one another. The joints are to be coated with quicklime [a powdery by-product of limestone] worked up with oil.[38]

THE PUBLIC FOUNTAINS

Whether they were made of lead or ceramics, pipes radiated outward from the distribution building, carrying the aqueduct's water to different parts of the town. These pipes were usually buried about two feet beneath the pavement. Another problem had to be overcome before the water reached its final destinations, though, related to the fact that forcing water into a small pipe and slanting the pipe downward to take advantage of the force of gravity creates increasing pressure within the pipe. If this pressure is left unchecked, either the pipe will burst at one of its seams or the water will gush out of the end of the pipe in an unmanageable torrent. To solve this problem, engineers built a series of hollow stone or brick columns at intervals within the town. Inside each column, the incoming water pipes rose straight up for several feet, helping to reduce the pressure, and emptied into a tank at the top. From the tank, the water entered and flowed down a set of outgoing pipes, which led to the precious liquid's final destinations.

Of these destinations, the public fountains received the largest share of water from the aqueducts. These fountains were not primarily decorative in purpose, as most fountains are today; instead, they were where most urban dwellers got their daily supplies of water for drinking and cooking. There were two reasons why most people did not have running water within their own homes. First, most of the inhabitants of Rome and other large cities lived in multistoried apartment blocks (the *insulae*). Some of the shops and apartments on the ground floors of these buildings did have running water piped in; but the water pressure at this point in the system was much too low to supply the upper floors.

Also, as a rule, running lines from the aqueducts directly to private homes was forbidden by law. The exceptions were the houses

of emperors, senators, military leaders, and other noble or highly placed individuals, who often did have their own private water lines, ending in sinks equipped with bronze faucets not much different than those in modern kitchens and bathrooms. Owners of large businesses and a few others were also sometimes granted special permission to receive aqueduct water privately. According to Frontinus, "No one shall draw water from the public supply without a license. . . . Whoever wishes to draw water for private use must seek for a grant and bring to the commissioner a writing [official permit] from the emperor."[39]

The vast majority of people had no chance of receiving such special permission, however. So most city dwellers had to make do with walking to the nearest fountain, filling up their buckets, and trudging home. To make this chore as painless as possible, public

Much aqueduct water went to public baths, like the Baths of Caracalla, shown here.

fountains were usually placed no more than 260 feet apart. This way, every person had access to clean aqueduct water within a radius of about 130 feet of his or her home.

THE PROBLEM OF WATER THEFT

Although the law forbade private use of the water from the aqueducts, except by a privileged few or by special government permit, many people ignored the law and proceeded to divert water from these channels for their private use. At times this involved the illicit cooperation of maintenance workers and other members of the water commission; at least some of these individuals were apparently not above supplementing their regular incomes with bribes from people living in areas near the aqueducts. The problem of water theft was serious and widespread, as Frontinus discovered when he carefully inspected the aqueducts shortly after becoming water commissioner. "There is fraud" in the water delivery system, he duly reported,

> since the amount actually delivered does not agree either with the statements of the records or the [measurements] made by us at the intake [start of the aqueduct], or even those made at the settling-basins. The cause of this is the dishonesty of the water-men [hired by former water commissioners], whom we have detected diverting water from the public conduits for private use. But a large number of landowners also, past whose fields the aqueducts run, tap the conduits. . . . We have found irrigated fields, shops, garrets [houses of prostitution] even, and lastly . . . [private] houses fitted up with fixtures through which a constant supply of flowing water might be assured.[40]

Frontinus then cites some specific examples of the "intolerable" methods used by water commission workers to cheat the system:

> When a water-right [the legal right to divert water for private use] is transferred to a new owner, they will insert a new nozzle in the reservoir; the old one they leave in the tank and draw from it water which they sell [illegally]. This practice especially . . . should be corrected by the Commissioner. . . . The following mode of gaining money, practiced by the water-men, is also to be abolished—the one called "puncturing." There are extensive areas in various places where secret pipes run under the pavements all over the city [of Rome]. I discovered that these pipes are furnishing water by special branches to all those engaged in business in those localities through which the pipes ran, being bored [drilled] for that purpose here and there by the so-called "puncturers." . . . How large an amount of water has been stolen in this manner, I estimate by means of the fact that a considerable quantity of lead has been brought in by the removal [at Frontinus's order] of that kind of [illegal] branch pipes.[41]

A long-standing, well-worded law on the books punished such fraud; the penalty demanded that a violator pay a stiff fine— of 100,000 *sesertii*, about one hundred times the annual salary of an average Roman soldier—plus repair any damage to the aqueducts he or she had caused. (If a slave committed the crime, his or her master had to pay the fine.) Frontinus was well aware that this law was by no means a strong deterrent against water theft; he recommended constant vigilance by the water commissioner and his staff as one effective way to combat the problem:

> Frequent rounds must be made of the channels of the aqueducts outside the city and with great care, to check up [on] the granted quantities [of water]. The same must be done in the case of reservoirs and public fountains, that the water may flow without interruption, day and night.[42]

Just how effective Frontinus and his successors were at reducing the amount of water stolen from the aqueducts is unknown.

THE PENALTY FOR TAMPERING WITH THE AQUEDUCTS

In his *Aqueducts of Rome*, Frontinus cites a law, excerpted here, dealing with those who purposely and illegally tampered with or damaged the aqueducts, including water thieves.

> Whoever, after the passage of this law, shall maliciously and intentionally pierce, break, or countenance [approve or tolerate] the attempt to pierce or break the channels, conduits, arches, pipes, tubes, reservoirs, or basins of the public waters . . . or who shall do damage with intent to prevent watercourses, or any portions of them, from going, falling, flowing, reaching, or being conducted into the city of Rome . . . shall be condemned to pay a fine of 100,000 *sestertii* to the Roman people; and in addition, whoever shall maliciously do any of these things shall be condemned to repair, restore, reestablish, reconstruct, [or] replace what he has damaged and quickly demolish what he has built [to convey stolen water]—all in good faith and in such manner as the [water] commissioners may determine. Further, whoever is or shall be water commissioner . . . is authorized to fine, bind over by bail, or restrain the offender.

MAINTENANCE AND REPAIR

Checking for fraud was just one aspect of the regular aqueduct maintenance Frontinus performed as water commissioner. "The necessity of repairs arises from the following reasons," he wrote:

> Damage is done either by the lawlessness of landowners living along the aqueducts, by age, by violent storms, or by defects in the original construction, which has happened quite frequently in the case of recent works. . . . Defects are either of the sort that can be remedied without stopping the flow of the water, or such as cannot be made without diverting the flow, as, for example, those which have to be made in the channel itself. The latter become necessary from two causes: either the accumulation of deposit, which sometimes hardens into a crust, contracts [narrows] the channel of the water; or else the concrete lining is damaged, causing leaks, whereby the sides of the conduits and the substructures are necessarily injured.[43]

Augustus's friend, Marcus Agrippa, who served as Rome's first water commissioner.

Frontinus then goes on to explain which seasons are best for each sort of repair job. For example, fixing the *specus* itself, he says, should not be attempted in the summer, since this is the season of peak demand for water. And if the flow of water absolutely must be diverted to repair the water channel, he warns, "a single aqueduct must be repaired at a time, for if several were cut off at once, the supply would prove inadequate for the city's needs."[44]

The vast majority of aqueduct maintenance and repair was done by specially trained brigades of slaves. The water commission had been created about a century before Frontinus's time by the first emperor, Augustus, who had appointed his friend Marcus Agrippa to head it. According to Frontinus, Agrippa kept his own private gang of slaves for the maintenance of the aqueducts and reservoirs and basins. This gang was [later] given to the state as its property by Augustus, who had received it in inheritance from Agrippa. . . . There are [now] two of those gangs, one belonging to the state, the other to Caesar [i.e., the current emperor, whomever he may be]. The one belonging to the state is the older. . . . It numbers about 240 men. The number in Caesar's gang is 460; it was organized by [the emperor] Claudius [reigned 41–54] at the time that he brought his aqueduct [the Aqua Claudia] into the city.[45]

Next, Frontinus tells how each slave gang was divided into specialized groups, including managers, inspectors, and various kinds of craftsmen to make any necessary repairs. During an emergency, he says, these extremely well drilled workers rushed into action, diverting water from various regions of the city to the region in need. Frontinus also mentions how the slaves in these gangs were paid.

Both gangs are divided into several classes of workmen: overseers, reservoir-keepers, inspectors, pavers, plasterers and other workmen; of these, some must be outside the city [Rome] for purposes which do not seem to require any great amount of work, but yet demand prompt attention; the men inside the city at their stations at the reservoirs and fountains will devote their energies to the several works, especially in cases of sudden emergencies, in order that a plentiful reserve supply of water may be turned from several wards of the city to the one afflicted by an emergency. . . . The wages of the state gang are paid from the state treasury, an expense which is lightened by the receipt of rentals from water-rights, which are received from places or buildings situated near the conduits, reservoirs, public fountains, or water-basins. This income of nearly 250,000 *sestertii*, formerly lost through loose management, was turned in recent times into the coffers of [the emperor] Domitian; but with a due sense of right [the emperor] Nerva restored it to the people. . . . The gang of Caesar gets its wages from the emperor's privy purse [imperial finance office], from which are also drawn all expenses for lead [for pipes] and for conduits, reservoirs, and basins [that make up the system of aqueducts].[46]

THE END OF ROME'S AQUEDUCTS

Sextus Julius Frontinus died about A.D. 104, just a few years after completing his book about the Roman aqueducts. After that, only two more aqueducts were built for the capital city—the Aqua Traiana (109) and the Aqua Alexandriana (206). Over time, the focus of power shifted within the Roman Empire, a series of events that indirectly affected the aqueducts. In 330, the emperor Constantine I established an eastern capital at Constantinople (on the Bosphorus strait), and in 404 the emperor Honorius moved the western capital from Rome to Ravenna (in northeastern Italy). So Rome lost some of its importance and also some of its population, which meant that its need for water lessened. Not only were no more new aqueducts built, but the existing ones increasingly fell into disrepair, especially after the year 500. (By this time, the old Roman government was gone, the last emperor having been de-

The emperor Constantine I, rendered in this bust, built a new Roman capital in the East.

posed in 476, and Germanic kings were ruling the city and the pitiful remnants of its formerly great realm.)

As the centuries wore on, some of the aqueducts were occasionally repaired by the impoverished medieval residents of Rome, but this work was haphazard and inadequate. And all eleven of these once marvelous structures had completely shut down by the eleventh century. Like their distant ancestors, most of the people now had to rely on the muddy waters of the Tiber River for drinking, cooking, and washing. For Rome and its water supply, the wheel had come full circle.

I 5

Bridges for the Roads and Aqueducts

To carry roads and aqueducts over various natural obstacles, the Romans needed bridges. And just as they did in many other areas of engineering and construction, they became very adept at the art of bridge building. Incredibly, some of the thousands of bridges they built fully two millennia ago are still in use today and daily bear with ease the tremendous weight of hundreds of modern cars, trucks, and buses. The challenges Roman engineers overcame to construct such useful and enduring structures

This Roman bridge, one of many that are beautifully preserved, was erected over the Rio Guadiana in Merida, Spain, in the late first century B.C.

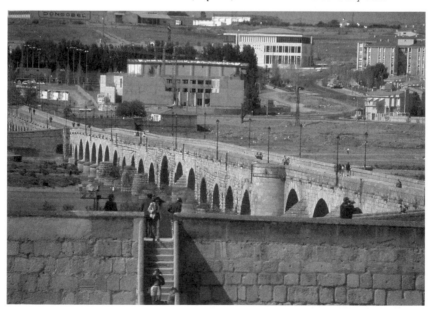

were daunting; had they built nothing else, their bridges alone would rank them among history's most accomplished builders. As Colin O'Connor puts it:

> To build a bridge is not merely an academic exercise—rather it is a practical task whose magnitude will vary with the size of the bridge. It is an exercise in management and logistics and, in a sense, it is also a conflict, as a bridge builder must contend with certain major forces of nature. It requires him to overcome the force of gravity—to handle major lifts that can be a frightening experience—and in many structures to counter the savage effects caused by a stream in flood. It requires not only immediate success, but a success that will last. How then should Roman bridge construction be assessed? As one of the most successful, extensive, and lasting of all human, material achievements.[47]

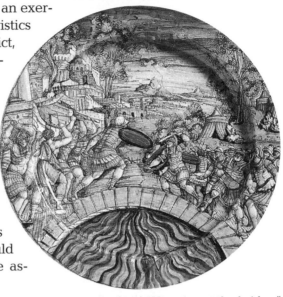

The legendary episode of "Horatius at the bridge" is depicted on this ancient plate.

WOODEN BRIDGES

Some Roman bridges, including all of the earliest versions, were made of wood. Perhaps the most famous early bridge was the Pons Sublicius, which led across the Tiber River and into Rome. First erected in the seventh or sixth century B.C., when Rome was still a small state ruled by local kings, it played a pivotal part in one of the Romans' most cherished heroic legends. In about 508 B.C., when an Etruscan army was attacking Rome, so the story goes, a Roman soldier called Horatius the One-Eyed single-handedly held off the invaders while his friends demolished the bridge behind him, thus saving the city. Afterward, Roman engineers supposedly rose to the task and designed the bridge's replacement so that it could be dismantled quickly when attackers threatened. Over the years, timber bridges, some built by and for the army and others erected by local towns and individuals, appeared by the hundreds throughout Italy and other Roman territories. They spanned streams, rivers, gorges, and other obstacles and became regular features of Rome's growing road network.

The standard procedure for building a timber bridge was to drive large vertical piles into the ground or riverbed. This work

CAESAR'S BRIDGE SPANS THE RHINE

This is Julius Caesar's description (from Rex Warner's translation of Caesar's *Commentary on the Gallic War*) of the building of a wooden military bridge over the Rhine River in 55 B.C.

Two piles, eighteen inches thick, slightly pointed at the lower ends and of lengths varying in accordance with the depth of the river, were fastened together two feet apart; they were then lowered into the river from rafts, fixed firmly in the river-bed, and driven home with piledrivers. Instead of being driven in vertically, as piles usually are, they were fixed obliquely [at an angle], leaning in the direction of the current. Opposite these again, and forty feet downstream, another pair of piles was fixed and coupled together in the same way, though this time they slanted forward against the force of the current. The two pairs of piles were then joined by a beam, two feet wide, the ends of which fitted exactly into the spaces between the two piles of each pair. The pairs were kept apart from each other by braces which secured each pile to the end of the cross-beam. The piles were thus both held apart and, in a different sense, clamped together. The whole structure was strong and so adapted to the forces of nature that the greater the strength of the current, the more tightly locked were the timbers. A series of these trestles was pushed across the river. They were connected with each other by timbers set at right angles, on top of which were laid poles and bundles of sticks. . . . Ten days after we had started to collect the timber, the whole work had been finished and the army led across.

was accomplished by piledrivers, machines consisting of heavy weights that were maneuvered up and down by means of pulley systems. When necessary, the tips of the piles were sheathed in iron so that they would not be worn down and weakened as workers pounded them in. Once these vertical supports, or piers, were in place, horizontal beams were attached to them, forming a trestle (a firmly braced framework); the trestle provided the support for the beams and wooden planks that formed the roadway used by people, animals, and wagons.

Although some such timber bridges were small, befitting their needs (crossing a narrow stream, for example), some were quite impressive engineering works. A famous example is the bridge that the renowned military general Julius Caesar built across the Rhine River (on the border between Gaul and Germany) in 55 B.C. About forty feet wide, some fifteen hundred feet long, and erected in just ten days, it was meant to intimidate the Germans by showing them that the Romans could cross over into their territory any time they pleased. Fortunately for modern scholars, Caesar described the construction of this bridge in his military journal (the *Commentary on the Gallic War*). "Two piles," he begins,

> eighteen inches thick, slightly pointed at the lower ends and of lengths varying in accordance with the depth of the river, were fastened together two feet apart; they were then lowered into the river from rafts, fixed firmly in the river-bed, and driven home with piledrivers.[48]

After giving more details, Caesar brags: "The whole structure was strong and so adapted to the forces of nature that the greater the strength of the current, the more tightly locked were the timbers."[49]

LAYING THE FOUNDATIONS AND PIERS

Caesar had good reason to be proud of an achievement of the stature of the Rhine River bridge. However, he was well aware that wooden bridges, no matter how well built and strong, were ultimately temporary, for wood rots and weakens over time. He had chosen wood because, for strategic purposes, he needed to create a bridge very quickly and with whatever materials were most plentiful in the area; but by his day, the Romans had already been constructing more permanent bridges out of masonry (stone or brick)

The spectacular remains of the multiple arches of a Roman viaduct (a masonry arcade supporting a roadway) dominate this view of a valley in Spain.

for over two centuries. Many, erected for both roads and aqueducts, consisted of the elegant rows of arches (arcades) that have become a familiar Roman trademark. Arcades supporting roadways are also referred to as viaducts. (Not all bridges were arcades, however; smaller masonry bridges might consist of only one arch.)

Construction of Roman masonry bridges followed a roughly standard series of steps. The first step was to provide a firm foundation for the piers, which in these structures, of course, were made of stone rather than wood. The ideal situation was one in which the terrain beneath the bridge was composed of solid rock, in which case the foundation was ready-made, so to speak; but more often than not, and especially when the terrain was submerged, the ground was soft and the builders had to fabricate a proper foundation.

Such foundations were most often composed of concrete. The Greeks had long before learned to mix lime, sand, and water to produce a hard-drying mortar and they had passed this knowledge on to the Romans. It did not take long for the latter, with their usual sense of practicality, to improve on the idea. Sometime in the third century B.C., Roman builders discovered that adding a special kind of sand to lime, in a ratio of two or three to one, produced a cement of rocklike hardness and great strength. Moreover, this new kind of concrete hardened underwater, which made it ideal for building bridges over rivers.

ROMAN SCAFFOLDING

Historian Jean-Pierre Adam gives the following description (in *Roman Building: Materials and Techniques*) of Roman scaffolding, used in building tall structures, including bridges.

In the case of both large construction and masonry, scaffolding remained a light structure, simply intended to support the workmen, their tools and small-size material; neither lifting machines nor heavy blocks could be placed on it. The wood used in its construction was therefore fairly small in section: poles, logs and planks. . . . Freestanding scaffolding had to support itself and of necessity rested on the ground. . . . The vertical supports were long pieces of wood simply stripped and retaining their natural shape, called standards. . . . At regular heights, depending on the requirements of the work, horizontal pieces joined two scaffolding poles to one another; the long longitudinal pieces (parallel to the wall) are the ledgers; the ones at right angles and supporting the  boards, are the putlogs or putlocks. The whole thing is made stable by the diagonal pieces of bracing . . . and by sloping props resting on the ground. . . . To economize on wood, while still guaranteeing complete stability . . . the Roman builders frequently used socketed scaffolding, which replaced the support of the poles with the masonry itself. As they progressed up the wall, the workmen carefully made a series of holes . . . aligned at the same horizontal level and in which they placed the ends of the putlogs.

Found near Mt. Vesuvius and other volcanoes, the sand in question was actually volcanic ash laid down in prehistoric eruptions. Because the main source of the material was Puteoli, on Vesuvius's slopes, the mortar it produced came to be called *pulvis Puteolanus*. The modern term "mortar" derives from the *mortarium*, the wooden trough in which Roman masons mixed the volcanic sand and lime with water. They made the concrete by mixing wet *pulvis Puteolanus* with coarse sand and gravel. The usual method was to lay down a layer of wet mortar, press in a layer of gravel, lay down more mortar, add another level of gravel, and so on, until they had achieved the desired thickness.

Once the solid concrete foundation had been laid (if needed), the next step was to erect the piers above it. In the case of bridges that rose on dry land, this was a fairly straightforward process; however, when a bridge crossed over a river or other waterway, the water had to be removed from the work area before either of these steps could be effectively accomplished. The builders managed this seemingly formidable task using a fairly simple and quite effective device called a coffer dam. This was, in essence, a large wooden box that had no top or bottom and whose sides had been sealed to ensure that it was watertight. Workers lowered the box into the water in the place where they desired to place a pier, pushing the wood firmly into the riverbed and making sure that the sides of the box rose several feet above the water's surface. Then they pumped out the water that was trapped inside the dam. For this task, "in most cases buckets or a bucket-chain would be adequate," write the Hameys:

> The waterscrew, or Archimedean screw [a corkscrewlike device that carried water upward when it was turned] was particularly useful, as it is today, since it could be turned by slaves working on dry land or in a barge tied up alongside the coffer-dam.[50]

When the ground inside the dam was dry, the workers laid the concrete foundation and began building the pier. Once the pier was higher than the water level outside the dam, the workers removed the dam and stood on scaffolding attached to the pier itself to finish its construction.

ARCHES AND ARCADES

When the bridge's piers reached the desired height, it was time to join them together with graceful, sweeping stone arches.

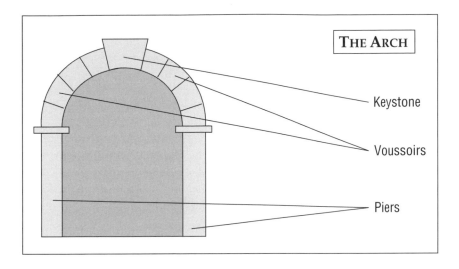

THE ARCH

Keystone

Voussoirs

Piers

Each arch was composed of two arcs (curved lines) of wedge-shaped stones, known as voussoirs (voo-SWARS), which met each other at a central stone, the keystone, at the top. The natural question is: How did the masons manage to keep the wedges from falling while the arch was under construction? They did so using a temporary support called "centering"; this was a sturdy timber framework that carpenters fashioned into a semicircle that fit exactly into the semicircular space directly below the arch. The centering bore the great weight of the stone wedges until the keystone was in place. Then the workers removed the centering, allowing the weight of the stones to be displaced, as intended, through the curve of the arch itself.

The last step in building a bridge was to construct the roadway or water channel atop the completed arches. But before this could be accomplished, the builders had to be satisfied that the structure was tall enough to meet the requirements of the specific situation. If the height of the completed piers and arches was deemed sufficient, the road or *specus* was laid in place, finishing the bridge. On the other hand, if more height was needed, one or more additional arcades could be built on top of the first one. The Roman aqueduct arcade still standing at Segovia, in north-central Spain, for example, has such a two-tier arrangement. (This magnificent structure, which is 2,388 feet long and 95 feet high, supports a water channel that is still in use, carrying water to the town from a stream some eleven miles distant.)

Another bridge, perhaps the most famous of all those built by the Romans, has a three-tiered arrangement of arcades. This is the Pont du Gard, which crosses a deep valley near Nimes, in southern France (formerly Roman Gaul). Interestingly, this bridge is an excellent surviving example not only of multiple arcades, but also of a bridge that supported both a roadway and an aqueduct. The tops of the bottom two tiers, roughly twenty and fifteen feet wide, respectively, were paved and supported pedestrian traffic; the narrower topmost tier carried a section of the *specus* of an aqueduct with a total length of some thirty-one miles.

MEMORIALS TO THE ROMAN ACHIEVEMENT

The Pont du Gard, which has stood, splendid and resolute, for some twenty centuries, also serves as an eternal memorial to the engineers and workers, both free and slave, who labored to erect

THE PONT DU GARD

This description of the famous Roman bridge built near Nimes (called Nemausus in ancient times), in southern France, is by engineer and historian Colin O'Connor, from his book *Roman Bridges*.

The Pont du Gard . . . forms part of an aqueduct which carries [water] to Nimes [over] a distance of some 50 km [31 miles], with a fall [difference in elevation between start and finish] of 17 m [56 feet]. . . . Although there is some doubt concerning its origin, the commonly accepted view is that it was built by Marcus Vipsanius Agrippa [Augustus's friend and adviser] about the year 18 B.C. . . . The bridge is constructed in three tiers, with the two lower tiers . . . having equal spans. . . . The width of the structure varies, being about 6.0 m [20 feet] in tier one [the lowest one], 4.6 m [15 feet] in tier two, and 3.1 m [10 feet] in tier three. The water conduit is 1.25 m [4 feet] wide and 1.8 m [a little over 6 feet] high. It is roofed with stone. The main structure was built without mortar, excepting for that necessary to waterproof the conduit at the top.

The multiple levels and arches of the magnificent Pont du Gard, in southern France (formerly Roman Gaul), exemplify Rome's great achievement in building roads, aqueducts, and bridges.

it. This mighty structure, along with the Via Appia, Aqua Marcia, and the thousands of other Roman bridges, roads, and aqueducts whose remains grace cities and countrysides across the Mediterranean world, attests to the greatness of a vanished civilization. Perhaps the Romans, like other aggressive peoples in history, can be criticized for imposing their rule on others through the force of arms. But they must also be credited with bringing a remarkable degree of order, security, and civilized amenities, including their majestic system of roads and aqueducts, to the areas they conquered. Writing in the second century A.D., when the Roman Empire was at its height, a representative of one of those conquered peoples, the Greek writer Aelius Aristides, could only praise the Roman achievement:

> Every place is full of gymnasia, fountains, gateways, temples, shops, and schools. . . . Cities shine in radiance and beauty, and the entire countryside is decked out like

a pleasure ground. Only those outside your Empire, if there are any, are fit to be pitied for losing such blessings. . . . [Using the Roman roads] Greek and non-Greek can now readily go wherever they please, with their property or without it. . . . You have surveyed the whole world, built bridges of all sorts across rivers, cut down mountains to make paths . . . filled the deserts with hostels, and civilized it all with system and order.[51]

Ⅰ NOTES

Introduction

1. Edith Hamilton, *The Roman Way to Western Civilization.* New York: W. W. Norton, 1932, p.116.
2. Hamilton, *Roman Way*, p. 116.
3. Lionel Casson, *Travel in the Ancient World.* Baltimore: Johns Hopkins University Press, 1994, p. 163.
4. Colin O'Connor, *Roman Bridges.* Cambridge, England: Cambridge University Press, 1993, p. 4.
5. O'Connor, *Roman Bridges*, p. 150.
6. Jean-Pierre Adam, *Roman Building: Materials and Techniques.* Trans. Anthony Mathews. Bloomington: Indiana University Press, 1994, p. 284.

Chapter 1: How the Romans Constructed Their Roads

7. Herodotus, *The Histories.* Trans. Aubrey de Sélincourt. New York: Penguin, 1972, pp. 359–60.
8. Casson, *Travel*, p. 163.
9. Quoted in Raymond Chevallier, *Roman Roads.* Trans. N. H. Field. Berkeley and Los Angeles: University of California Press, 1976, p. 65.
10. Quoted in Chevallier, *Roman Roads*, pp. 65–66.
11. L. A. Hamey and J. A. Hamey, *The Roman Engineers.* Cambridge, England: Cambridge University Press, 1981, p. 21.
12. Casson, *Travel*, pp. 169–70.
13. Plutarch, *Life of Gaius Gracchus,* in *Lives of the Noble Grecians and Romans.* Trans. John Dryden. New York: Random House, 1932, p. 1012.

Chapter 2: Life and Customs Along the Roman Roads

14. Chevallier, *Roman Roads*, pp. 116–17.
15. Pliny the Elder, *Natural History,* excerpted in *Pliny the Elder: Natural History: A Selection.* Trans. John H. Healy. New York: Penguin, 1991, p. 182.
16. Livy, *The History of Rome from Its Foundation*, excerpted in *Livy: The War with Hannibal.* Trans. Aubrey de Sélincourt. New York: Penguin, 1972, p. 106.
17. Livy, *History of Rome*, excerpted in *Livy: The Early History of Rome.* Trans. Aubrey de Sélincourt. New York: Penguin, 1971, p. 314.

18. Livy, *History of Rome,* in *The War with Hannibal*, p. 365.

19. Casson, *Travel*, p. 183.

20. Casson, *Travel*, pp. 176–77.

21. Horace, *Satires*, quoted in Jo-Ann Shelton, ed., *As the Romans Did: A Sourcebook in Roman Social History.* New York: Oxford University Press, 1988, pp. 327–28.

22. Quoted in Casson, *Travel*, p. 204.

23. Apuleius, *The Golden Ass.* Trans. P. G. Walsh. Oxford: Oxford University Press, 1994, p. 5.

24. Quoted in Casson, *Travel*, p. 223.

25. Apuleius, *Golden Ass*, Walsh translation, p. 148.

26. Apuleius, *Golden Ass*, Walsh translation, pp. 149–50.

Chapter 3: Building the Roman Aqueducts

27. Adam, *Roman Building*, p. 238.

28. Sextus Julius Frontinus, *The Aqueducts of Rome,* in *The Stratagems and the Aqueducts of Rome.* Trans. C. E. Bennett. Cambridge, MA: Harvard University Press, 1993, pp. 357–59.

29. Vitruvius, *On Architecture.* 2 vols. Trans. Frank Granger. Cambridge, MA: Harvard University Press, 1962, vol. 2, pp. 137–41.

30. Vitruvius, *On Architecture*, vol. 2, pp. 177–79.

31. Adam, *Roman Building*, pp. 241–42.

32. Hamey and Hamey, *Roman Engineers*, p. 15.

33. Quoted in L. Sprague de Camp, *The Ancient Engineers.* New York: Ballantine, 1963, pp. 207–208.

34. Vitruvius, *On Architecture*, vol. 2, p. 179.

Chapter 4: Water Distribution and Aqueduct Maintenance

35. Adam, *Roman Building*, p. 251.

36. De Camp, *Ancient Engineers*, p. 209.

37. Vitruvius, *On Architecture*, vol. 2, p. 189.

38. Vitruvius, *On Architecture*, vol. 2, p. 187.

39. Frontinus, *Aqueducts of Rome*, Bennett translation, pp. 433–37.

40. Frontinus, *Aqueducts of Rome*, Bennett translation, pp. 399, 405.

41. Frontinus, *Aqueducts of Rome*, Bennett translation, p. 447.

42. Frontinus, *Aqueducts of Rome*, Bennett translation, p. 435.

43. Frontinus, *Aqueducts of Rome*, Bennett translation, pp. 451–53.

44. Frontinus, *Aqueducts of Rome*, Bennett translation, p. 453.

45. Frontinus, *Aqueducts of Rome*, Bennett translation, pp. 427–29, 447–49.

46. Frontinus, *Aqueducts of Rome*, Bennett translation, pp. 449–51.

Chapter 5: Bridges for the Roads and Aqueducts

47. O'Connor, *Roman Bridges*, p. 188.

48. Julius Caesar, *Commentary on the Gallic War,* in *War Commentaries of Caesar*. Trans. Rex Warner. New York: New American Library, 1960, p. 78.

49. Caesar, *Commentary*, Warner translation, p. 78.

50. Hamey and Hamey, *Roman Engineers*, p. 32.

51. Aelius Aristides, *Roman Panegyric,* quoted in Naphtali Lewis and Meyer Reinhold, eds., *Roman Civilization, Sourcebook II: The Empire*. New York: Harper and Row, 1966, p. 138.

GLOSSARY

actus: Local roads, usually unpaved.

aediles: Roman officials in charge of maintaining public works and overseeing marketplaces and public games.

agger: A mound or embankment; or a road built atop a causeway.

agrimensores (or *librators*): Surveyors.

arch: An architectural form, usually curved in a semicircle, used to span the top of a door, window, bridge support, or other open space.

arcade: A row or continuous succession of arches; or a bridge utilizing such a row of arches.

atrium: A foyer or central hall.

castellum aquae: A water distribution building into which an aqueduct flowed and out of which pipes carried the water to various points in a town.

censors *(censores)*: Roman officials who conducted the census, oversaw public morality, decided on construction projects, and awarded contracts for such projects.

chorobates: A wooden device shaped like a bench, used by Roman surveyors to ensure that the ground or a structural foundation was level.

cippi: Milestones set up along the length of an aqueduct.

cistern: A reservoir for catching and storing rainwater.

coffer dam: A large boxlike device with no top or bottom that was lowered into a river or bay; once in place, workers pumped out the water caught inside the box so that they could more easily lay the foundation of a bridge or other structure.

compluvium: An opening in the roof through which rainwater flowed down into a basin (*impluvium*).

curator aquarum: A water commissioner, charged with maintaining a city's water supply, including its aqueducts.

curatores viarum: A board of officials set up by the emperor Augustus to manage public highways in Italy.

cursus clabularis: An official military transport service set up by the emperor Septimius Severus.

cursus publicus: "Government post"; an official courier service set up by the emperor Augustus.

dioptra: A surveying instrument that could be used to determine differences in elevation between two points.

impluvium: A catchbasin, situated on the floor directly beneath an opening in the roof (*compluvium*), for storing rainwater.

insulae: Apartment buildings or blocks.

itineraria: Itineraries; road books that listed towns, inns, and other stops along the major roads.

keystone: The central, topmost voussoir in an arch.

ledgers: In Roman scaffolding, the horizontal planks running parallel to the wall in front of which the scaffolding was erected; the workers stood on the ledgers.

mansiones: Inns along the roads, at first used by the couriers of the *cursus publicus*, but later by the general public.

masonry: Stone or brick.

miliaria: Milestones set up at intervals of a Roman mile along the major roads.

miliarium aureum: "Golden milestone"; a special milestone, inscribed with the distances to many other locations, set up in the city of Rome.

mortarium: A wooden trough in which masons mixed mortar.

mutationes: Posting stations on major roads, where couriers and others obtained fresh horses or mules, as well as spare parts for carriages and carts.

pier: A vertical support for an arch.

piscinae limariae: Settling tanks in which water was stored long enough for any sediment to settle to the bottom.

privatae: Private roads maintained by one or more landowners.

pulvis Puteolanus: The mortar used in making Roman concrete; named after the town of Puteoli (near Mt. Vesuvius), the main source of the volcanic ash that constituted its main ingredient.

puteus: A vertical shaft dug into the earth; or a well; or a prison.

putlogs (or putlocks): In Roman scaffolding, the horizontal supports running at right angles to the wall in front of which the scaffolding was erected; sometime the inner ends of the putlogs were inserted into holes in the wall for extra support.

reda: A four-wheeled carriage.

speculatores: Military scouts who manned the *cursus publicus.*

specus: The water channel constituting the heart of an aqueduct.

standards: The vertical supports in the wooden scaffolding used by Roman builders.

taberna: An inn, in particular one that served wine and food; or a shop; or a hut.

trestle: In a bridge, a framework (made of wood or some other material) used to support a roadway.

via: A road.

viaduct: A row of arches supporting a roadway.

via glarea strata: A road surfaced in gravel.

via silice strata: A road paved with stone.

via terena: A dirt road.

viae militares: Roads originally built and used by the army.

viae publicae: Public highways.

vicus: A city street.

voussoir: One of several individual wedge-shaped elements that form the curve of an arch.

FOR FURTHER READING

Ian Andrews, *Pompeii*. Cambridge, England: Cambridge University Press, 1978. A colorfully illustrated volume summarizing the story of the town's volcanic burial, its rediscovery, and its main points of interest for scholars and tourists.

Isaac Asimov, *The Roman Empire*. Boston: Houghton Mifflin, 1967. A well-written general synopsis of Roman civilization in imperial times.

Anthony Marks and Graham Tingay, *The Romans*. London: Usborne, 1990. An excellent summary of the main aspects of Roman history, life, and arts, supported by hundreds of beautiful and accurate drawings reconstructing Roman times. Aimed at basic readers but highly recommended for anyone interested in Roman civilization.

Claude Moatti, *In Search of Ancient Rome*. New York: Harry N. Abrams, 1993. This beautifully illustrated book effectively summarizes the main discoveries made by archaeologists and art historians in Roman Italy.

Don Nardo, *The Age of Augustus*. San Diego: Lucent Books, 1996. This and the following four volumes by the same author are comprehensive but easy-to-read overviews of various aspects of the civilization that produced Rome's systems of roads and aqueducts. They provide a broader context for understanding the leaders, trends, ideas, themes, and events of Roman history.

———, *The Decline and Fall of the Roman Empire*. San Diego: Lucent Books, 1998.

———, *Games of Ancient Rome*. San Diego: Lucent Books, 2000.

———, *Greek and Roman Mythology*. San Diego: Lucent Books, 1997.

———, *Greek and Roman Sport*. San Diego: Lucent Books, 1999.

Jonathon Rutland, *See Inside a Roman Town*. New York: Barnes and Noble, 1986. A very attractively illustrated introduction to major concepts of Roman civilization for basic readers.

Judith Simpson, *Ancient Rome*. New York: Time-Life, 1997. One of the latest entries in Time-Life's library of picture books about the ancient world, this one is beautifully illustrated with attractive and appropriate photographs and paintings. The general but well-written text is aimed at intermediate readers.

Works Consulted

Ancient Sources:

Apuleius, *The Golden Ass*. Trans. P. G. Walsh. Oxford: Oxford University Press, 1994. The only complete Roman novel that has survived.

Julius Caesar, *Commentary on the Gallic War,* in *War Commentaries of Caesar*. Trans. Rex Warner. New York: New American Library, 1960. Contains the great general's own description of his feats, including building a bridge over the Rhine River.

Sextus Julius Frontinus, *The Stratagems and the Aqueducts of Rome*. Trans. C. E. Bennett. Cambridge, MA: Harvard University Press, 1993. Frontinus, water commissioner for the city of Rome in the late first century A.D., left behind this priceless compendium of facts about the aqueducts supplying the Empire's capital.

Herodotus, *The Histories*. Trans. Aubrey de Sélincourt. New York: Penguin, 1972. This treasure trove of information about the eastern Mediterranean peoples of the author's day has several references to engineering feats, including the Persian road system.

Naphtali Lewis and Meyer Reinhold, eds., *Roman Civilization, Sourcebook II: The Empire*. New York: Harper and Row, 1966. A large and extremely useful collection of ancient documents.

Livy, *The History of Rome from Its Foundation*. Books 1–5 published as *Livy: The Early History of Rome*. Trans. Aubrey de Sélincourt. New York: Penguin, 1971; books 21–30 published as *Livy: The War with Hannibal*. Trans. Aubrey de Sélincourt. New York: Penguin, 1972. These sections of Livy's monumental history contain numerous references to soldiers and others using the Roman road system.

Pliny the Elder, *Natural History*, excerpted in *Pliny the Elder: Natural History: A Selection*. Trans. John H. Healy. New York: Penguin, 1991. Among the many topics Pliny tackles in this huge compendium of facts about his world is water—how to find it, wells, water distribution, and so forth.

Plutarch, *Parallel Lives*, published complete as *Lives of the Noble Grecians and Romans*. Trans. John Dryden. New York: Random House, 1932; also excerpted in *Fall of the Roman Republic: Six Lives by Plutarch*. Trans. Rex Warner. New York: Penguin, 1972; and *Makers of Rome: Nine Lives by Plutarch*. Trans. Ian Scott-Kilvert. New York: Penguin, 1965. Writing in the late first century A.D., Plutarch, a Romanized Greek biographer and moralist, had access to many ancient documents now lost, making his works extremely valuable to modern historians.

Seneca, assorted works in *Seneca: Dialogues and Letters*. Trans. C. D. N. Costa. New York: Penguin, 1997. Seneca was a brilliant, witty, urbane philosopher, playwright, and for a time an adviser to the notorious emperor Nero.

Jo-Ann Shelton, ed., *As the Romans Did: A Sourcebook in Roman Social History*. New York: Oxford University Press, 1988. An excellent collection of ancient Roman documents, with much useful commentary by Shelton, a fine scholar.

Statius, *Silvae*. Trans. K. M. Coleman. Oxford: Oxford University Press, 1988. Statius was a poet who enjoyed the patronage of the emperor Domitian. The *Silvae* contains a description of the building of a road.

Suetonius, *Lives of the Twelve Caesars*, published as *The Twelve Caesars*. Trans. Robert Graves, rev. Michael Grant. New York: Penguin, 1979. This Roman historian's biographies of Roman notables contain much valuable information about the people and events of the late Republic and early Empire.

Vitruvius, *On Architecture*. 2 vols. Trans. Frank Granger. Cambridge, MA: Harvard University Press, 1962. This work, summarizing basic knowledge on architecture, engineering, water supplies, and other subjects, had a profound influence on architects in the European Renaissance.

Major Modern Sources:

Jean-Pierre Adam, *Roman Building: Materials and Techniques*. Trans. Anthony Mathews. Bloomington: Indiana University Press, 1994. A large, comprehensive, authoritative study of all aspects of Roman building, including roads, aqueducts, and bridges. Also contains many fine photos and illustrations. Highly recommended.

Lionel Casson, *Daily Life in Ancient Rome*. New York: American Heritage Publishing, 1975. Casson, one of the finest and most popular classical scholars of the twentieth century, here provides an entertaining sketch of the basic aspects of Roman daily life.

———, *Travel in the Ancient World*. Baltimore: Johns Hopkins University Press, 1994. A classic of its kind, Casson's study of ancient travelers and their conveyances includes fulsome sections on Roman roads and the facilities that grew up along them. This is fascinating, rewarding reading that brings the ancient world to life.

Raymond Chevallier, *Roman Roads*. Trans. N. H. Field. Berkeley and Los Angeles: University of California Press, 1976. A scholarly, somewhat haphazardly organized volume that is, nonetheless, the most comprehensive single study of Roman roads and a tremendously valuable resource.

L. Sprague de Camp, *The Ancient Engineers*. New York: Ballantine, 1963. This classic book is a fascinating compendium of information about ancient builders and their materials, techniques, and accomplishments. Highly recommended.

L. A. Hamey and J. A. Hamey, *The Roman Engineers*. Cambridge, England: Cambridge University Press, 1981. A short but very informative sketch of Roman building materials and techniques, this volume is distinctive for its helpful, well-rendered drawings of Roman workers engaged in constructing various projects.

Edith Hamilton, *The Roman Way to Western Civilization*. New York: W. W. Norton, 1932. One of the great historians of the twentieth century waxes poetic about the Romans—their character, thinking, faults, strengths, and achievements. Along with her companion work, *The Greek Way to Western Civilization*, a must for the well-rounded education.

William L. MacDonald, *The Architecture of the Roman Empire*. New Haven, CT: Yale University Press, 1982. A useful general source on ancient Roman architecture and building techniques.

Colin O'Connor, *Roman Bridges*. Cambridge, England: Cambridge University Press, 1993. The definitive modern source on Roman bridges, written by a noted bridge engineer who is also an excellent historian. Contains long, detailed sections on Roman roads, aqueducts, and the bridges that adorned them, along with appropriate photos and several useful lists and tables of statistics. Highly recommended for those interested in this subject.

J. B. Ward-Perkins, *Roman Imperial Architecture*. New York: Penguin, 1981. A very fine synopsis of Roman architectural styles, with numerous helpful photos of ruins from across the Mediterranean world.

ADDITIONAL MODERN SOURCES:

Lesley Adkins and Roy A. Adkins, *Handbook to Life in Ancient Rome*. New York: Facts On File, 1994.

Thomas Ashby, *The Aqueducts of Ancient Rome*. London: Oxford University Press, 1935.

J. P. V. D. Balsdon, *Life and Leisure in Ancient Rome*. New York: McGraw-Hill, 1969.

Matthew Bunson, *A Dictionary of the Roman Empire*. New York: Oxford University Press, 1995.

Jerome Carcopino, *Daily Life in Ancient Rome: The People and the City at the Height of the Empire*. New Haven, CT: Yale University Press, 1940.

Tim Cornell and John Matthews, *Atlas of the Roman World*. New York: Facts On File, 1982.

F. R. Cowell, *Life in Ancient Rome*. New York: G. P. Putnam's Sons, 1961.

Leonardo B. Dal Maso, *Rome of the Caesars*. Trans. Michael Hollingworth. Rome: Bonechi-Edizioni, n.d.

James K. Finch, *Engineering and Western Civilization*. New York: McGraw-Hill, 1951.

Ivor B. Hart, *The Great Engineers*. London: Methuen, 1928.

Richard S. Kirby et al., *Engineering in History*. New York: McGraw-Hill, 1956.

Senatore R. Lanciani, *Ancient and Modern Rome*. New York: Cooper Square, 1963.

Peter Quennell, *The Colosseum*. New York: Newsweek Book Division, 1971.

Chris Scarre, *Chronicle of the Roman Emperors*. London: Thames and Hudson, 1995.

Hans Straub, *A History of Civil Engineering*. London: L. Hill, 1952.

Mortimer Wheeler, *Roman Art and Architecture*. London: Thames and Hudson, 1964.

L. P. Wilkinson, *The Roman Experience*. Lanham, MD: University Press of America, 1974.

INDEX

PICTURE CREDITS

ABOUT THE AUTHOR

Historian Don Nardo has written numerous books about ancient Rome, among them *The Age of Augustus*, *The Punic Wars*, *Life of a Roman Soldier*, *The Decline and Fall of the Roman Empire*, *Games of Ancient Rome*, and a biography of Julius Caesar. Mr. Nardo also writes screenplays and teleplays and composes music. He lives with his wife, Christine, in Massachusetts.